CHATHAM TOWNSHIP, NJ:
SECRETS
FROM THE PAST

Ellie,   8/16/11
   It is with pleasure and
gratitude that I am sharing
this story with you. After all,
Inv was a constant source
of accurate information about
the Colony.

       Warmest regards and
       Best wishes.
       Bert

CHATHAM TOWNSHIP, NJ: SECRETS FROM THE PAST

THE RISE AND DEMISE OF AMERICA'S FOURTEENTH COLONY

BERT ABBAZIA

iUniverse, Inc.
Bloomington

Chatham Township, NJ: Secrets from the Past
The Rise and Demise of America's Fourteenth Colony

iUniverse books may be ordered through booksellers or by contacting:

iUniverse
1663 Liberty Drive
Bloomington, IN 47403
www.iuniverse.com
1-800-Authors (1-800-288-4677)

ISBN: 978-1-4620-2417-9 (sc)
ISBN: 978-1-4620-2418-6 (e)

Printed in the United States of America

iUniverse rev. date: 07/01/2011

THE RALLYING CRY
"WAKE UP- MY BROTHERS OF THE CITY!"

"YOU WORKERS WHO ARE SENTENCED, or have sentenced yourselves to live in the city all your lives- you have my sincere sympathy! You only half live!

All the magnitude and beauty of nature is overshadowed by the artificiality of "civilization." From sunrise to sundown all you see is artificiality and bliss. All the beauties of nature, all the thrills of creation, all the force of the storm don't exist for you. Why, you don't even see the getting up of the sun or the setting of it. They are all covered up by the dust and the smoke and the walls and the stones of the city.

How many of you ever see the beauty of the rising of the full moon without some chimney obstructing your view? How many of you smelled the waking-up earth in the spring, after a long winter's sleep? How many of you had their hearts throb at the sight of a chick coming out of a shell, or enjoyed the sight of the bud breaking into a flower, or have seen a newly born calf, or a lamb, or a colt? How many of you can hear the music in nature that no man can ever imitate? How many can see the beauty of color that no artist can ever paint? For what is art, if not an attempt to imitate the beauties and harmony of nature!

Wake, you brothers of the city! Come into the open! Learn to understand nature and she'll reward you a thousand fold! She'll pour a new meaning into your lives and fill it with joy and happiness that nothing else will surpass. She will teach you to understand each other, for you no longer know yourself and your own brothers. What you say you don't mean and what you mean you don't say.

Come into the open! Your lives will fill out! You will find yourself. You will learn to understand each other! All the beauties of art, and music and sculpture, and poetry will open to you if you only embrace Nature as she is. Come out and wake up!"

The preceding is the direct quote taken from The Chatham Colony News from May of 1924. The document expressed one man's hopes and dreams and aspirations for a small group of Eastern European immigrants seeking a better existence for their families and their fellow man. It was the road map for anyone who craved a life style of living in a natural environment, and enjoying all the benefits that nature could provide.

The man responsible for the document in the Colony News was Bernard Somer. Bernard was a young man in his early thirties with a gift and a power to organize and motivate people for causes that were Socialistic in nature. He could be likened to Joseph Smith, the founder and prime mover in the Mormon Religion. A, gentler, Joseph Smith with the similar zeal, passion and the ability to rally people for greater causes. He possessed the qualities of a leader. Somer turned out to be the right man, at the right time for those seeking a new beginning.

BACKGROUND

BERNARD WAS THE OLDEST OF three children born to Michael and Jeanette Somer in Bucharest Romania. Michael and Jeanette's other two children were daughters Sophie and Frieda. Bernard's early schooling included an apprenticeship as a book binder, at age eleven. He did not follow in the footsteps of his father, whose profession was that of a butcher. Sophie and Frieda took up sewing with the idea of one day becoming dressmakers. Both girls, during their early years, enjoyed formal schooling, along with their training as dressmakers. This was not unusual for many European children from families with modest means. Bernard grew up as a bright, spirited, energetic young man with grandiose ideas. To his immediate family and those who knew him best, Somer was thought of as a "Dreamer."

He had the mindset that the problems of the world could be solved by the organization of like-minded people striving for the same goals. Somer could best be described as a "Compassionate Socialist." His political views were shared by many Europeans. These were the political views of many who answered his call. The difference among them was one of degree. They ran the gamut from pacifists, socialists, communists to anarchists. In addition to their political views, they brought valuable skills and professional training to the new world. Somer, in his early efforts, assumed the title of "The Organizer."

RECRUTING A FOLLOWING

IN LOOKING BACK, THE CROSS-SECTION of people drawn to Somer's idealistic concept was predictable, because of the venue and the media he used in recruiting. He advertised for a following that would be sympathetic with his ideals and placed ads and articles in a local newspaper titled "The Call," which was a Socialist paper with a large readership among union members and union sympathizers. This group along with the readership of the Jewish New York paper "The Forward" reached a large network of people drawn to "The Organizer's" dream.

Somer, unwittingly, became the beneficiary from an unexpected source, the social clubs. Ethnic social clubs were "springing" up in Manhattan and Brooklyn and were becoming very popular with the new arrivals in America. The clubs offered a night of meeting and socializing with new people. The clubs became a place to meet people who spoke their language, to learn the latest dance steps, to hear about job opportunities, to find apartments, and most importantly provided a chance to learn and speak English. The clubs became their English 101 classroom. They exchanged ideas and experiences and developed relationships. One of these relationships ended in the marriage of a couple that became original Colony members. Frieda Somer married Oreste Abbazia and spent their entire lives at 208 now 252 Lafayette Avenue.

**Frieda and Oreste Abbazia met
at a New York social club.**

Bernard Somer's quest for a new and better future began in the late spring/early summer of 1921. The nucleus of people who shared the same convictions, religious views, political persuasion and a rural life style would be found in New York City. The City was teaming with immigrants from Europe. Boat loads of hard-working men and woman and entire families scraped together enough money to make the long, arduous, torturous trip across the Atlantic to an unknown land. A land of promise, and most compelling, a land of hope! Hope for a new and better life. America was HOPE!

THE SACRAFICE

THE UPROOTING OF FAMILIES WAS the supreme act of fulfilling one's personal convictions. The thought of facing the unknown was the ultimate life-changing experience for this idealistic group.

The hoards of people pouring into New York Harbor in the late 1890's, early 1900's represented a wide diversity of people from most, if not every, country in Europe. Although theses crusaders left their country of birth, they didn't leave their skills and professions behind, and most significantly, they brought their dreams. The range of their skills and professions was wide and diverse. The list included dressmakers, seamstresses, concert cellist, mechanic, haberdashery owner, bookbinder, optician, farmer, sculptor, carpenter, author, electrician, artist, plumber, dentist, teacher, newspaper editor, insurance broker, tailor, and a pioneer in the motion picture titles industry. This is a partial list of the skills and professions America inherited from these adventurous souls.

While some of the group were making new friends and acquaintances, it was not unusual to find that a few knew each other from the "old country." Some came from the same small village in Italy, some from the same province in Russia, some from the same city in Romania, and a couple had a casual encounter in France. In isolated instances some developed relationships that could best be described as "extended families." This applied to those immigrants who developed a relationship with a "friend of a friend," already residing in America. This group of idealists became the nucleus of the curious, the intrigued, the fascinated and those hungry for more information about a utopia that existed somewhere west of New York City. These were the Pilgrims of the 1890's and the early 1900's. These Pilgrims landed on Ellis Island instead of Plymouth Rock.

The amazing part was the number of individuals who, for one reason or another, were forced to make the long crossing alone. Most of those who were denied passage with their families were detained because of health reasons and improper paperwork. Thus, they were placed in quarantine until they were cleared for passage to America. It was not unusual for one or more in a family to be left behind and alone in a strange city, in a strange country. In some instances, those left behind were children. The sad and pathetic part was that in these cases, the children were as young as ten years old. They were stranded in a European port with little money, unable to speak the local language, and in the care of a foreign government. While these were isolated cases, they were, nevertheless, experienced by some of the families bent on coming to America. Bernard's eleven year old sister, Frieda, was a classic example of a child turned away at the dock for health reasons, the flu. Frieda was left alone in Paris, France, where she waited for her uncle to take her home to Bucharest to recover. Frieda did successfully get to America on her second attempt a few months later, alone!

THE MAGNET

THE SKYLINE OF NEW YORK City must have been a beacon and a magnet, as they migrated to four of the city's five boroughs. The Borough of Staten Island was too remote to attract the newcomers. Many settled in the crowded, steamy, push-cart jammed lower Eastside of Manhattan, while others for job and career opportunities made the Bronx their home. Others chose Brooklyn as an alternative to begin a new life. New York City provided all its new residents a chance to ply their trade, skills and professions, plus the ever-present feeling that the possibility of a better life existed between the Hudson and East rivers, and from the Bronx to the Battery.

The overwhelming majority did not own a car. The city, with its elevated trains, limited subway system, ferry boats and trolley cars made the need for private transportation an extravagant luxury. Every business and profession could be found in Manhattan. Brooklyn and the Bronx became the bedrooms of Manhattan. The workplace was within walking distance or a short commute via public transportation.

INTRODUCTION TO UTOPIA

SOMER'S FIRST BOOK BINDING JOB in America was with Dun and Bradstreet. His tenure at D & B was under five years. He was next employed by the Prudential Insurance Company jn Newark, New Jersey. He made Prudential his life time career as a bookbinder, and realized a comfortable living with a work schedule that allowed him to research and promote his dream.

Prudential was not only the source of his income, but also was the source of discovering his "utopia." Somer's search for his utopia took an unexpected twist in April/May 1921. The twist came in the form of a co-worker at the Prudential. Somer's colleague was a man by the name of Charlie Singawald. The Singawald Family were long-time residents of Chatham Township, New Jersey. Their homestead was a farm house on Lafayette Avenue, a street named after the French nobleman, the Marquis de Lafayette. While their modest home was set back forty feet from the road, apple trees covered their acres of property. Carved into the hill behind the house was a shed with a dirt floor and dirt walls. It was used for the storage of the apples and as a retail outlet to sell the apples. Eventually, the Singawalds sold not only apples, but also ice cream. Many people in the Township enjoyed their first Eskimo Pie at the Singawald shed. The Eskimo Pies were kept frozen with dry ice. For history buffs, the Singawald Homestead is now the site of Chatham High School, home of the Cougars.

Chatham Township in the 1920's was the boonies. It was "No Town, USA," no stores, no traffic lights, no medical facilities, no dentists, no movies, no lines in the street, no sidewalks, no pizza, no locks on doors. There were more cows and horses than there were cars. It seemed that the only color of cars was black. Township boys and some girls learned to skin a muskrat before they learned to drive a car. Chatham Township was Norman Rockwell's rural America.

It was during one of their on-going conversations at work, that Charlie Singawald described where he lived and how his family enjoyed the peace and quiet of the natural surroundings and the rural living. The more Charlie spoke, the more Somer realized Charlie was describing Somer's "utopia." Charlie now had Somer's undivided attention, when he mentioned a large tract of land across the street from his house was for sale. Charlie knew the name of the owner was a Mr. Estes but nothing more.

Somer quickly researched the Township tax map and found that the Estes's property extended from Pine Street to Southern Boulevard and from Lafayette Avenue to the easterly side of the Noe property, now Dale Drive. A small appendage to the property extended south of Southern Boulevard into what was referred to at the time, as the Great Swamp. For history buffs, boys living adjacent to this area enjoyed referring to one another as "Swampers".

AT LAST, UTOPIA

THE SWAMP WAS CONSIDERED A useless, worthless, piece of property. While it did have its own vast variety of vegetation and wild life, it was raw acreage that could never be developed. The swamp was home to deer, fox, raccoons, rabbits, squirrels, muskrats, skunks and weasels, plus many species of birds. Cardinals, robins, blue jays, wrens, hawks, blackbirds, oriels, owls, woodpeckers and countless other birds thrived in this gift of nature. Migrating ducks and wild geese made the swamp their annual stop-over on their way to and from their southerly destinations. Rarely seen snakes and lizards co-habited in this natural environment.

A first-time visitor had to be struck by the abundance of wild huckleberry bushes growing freely in and around the miles of swamp bogs. With the passage of time, the Great Swamp was designated as a National Wife Life Refuge. Young men still hunt deer and families take advantage of the observation areas and view its wonders up close. The generations from the 20's, 30's and 40's will always remember the Swamp as their Club Med. A key element in Somer's grandiose plan was now in motion. He was honing in on the prime tract of land that Charlie Singawald had introduced him to.

Who knew what Somer's thoughts and emotions were in the spring/summer of 1921 as he took his first step and meandered onto the untouched tract of land and began his exploration. He was now the "Lewis and Clark" of the East. Without any time constraints, Somer started his journey at the corner of Pine Street and Lafayette Avenue. He ambled leisurely around the trees and through the underbrush. Somer must have felt he was in an arboretum. His exploration took him under a variety of tall maple trees, giant oaks and silver grey birch trees. He had to be overwhelmed by the acres of white birch and white dogwood trees. Wild flowers decorated his path for the entire journey. Lily of the valley, wild red roses, yellow daffodils, pink lady slippers, purple violets, and red wild strawberries were all in evidence along the way. Some were still in bloom while others had concluded their annual show of colors. Somer, at this stage of his walk, became more relaxed since the terrain was relatively level. He was now in what would eventually become Maple Street and Floral Avenue. He did encounter gentle dips and slopes in his walk. The land dropped off as he approached the southerly part of the tract. This is now Spring Street.

The ground here became wet and soggy. Vegetation included brown cat-tails, marsh grass, swamp bogs and mossy green ground that covered the cold, clear water oozing from natural underground springs. This area was limited to two or three acres of wetlands, now the site of the Colony Club.

Somer continued his walk up a gradual rise in the terrain, where the texture of the soil seemed dry and sandier. He continued his exploration in a southerly direction. After crossing Southern Boulevard, he came upon acres and acres of marshy wetlands, covered by bogs, swamp grass and huckleberry bushes. Somer had come upon Nature's own huckleberry farm. He discovered the berries were as far as he could see. Somer's presence did not go unnoticed. Rabbits, squirrels, and an occasional deer crossed his path. He was an intruder in this paradise, very happy and an inspired intruder.

With each step Somer came to the realization that Chatham Township was his "Utopia". He had found the perfect environment for his family and friends. The birth of the Colony was in Phase one!

Although Chatham Township did become the eventual site of his utopian community, Somer had researched and explored Stelton New Jersey. It seems he had been a home owner in Stelton and had built a modest house that resembled a church. Stelton had many of the characteristics of Chatham Township in the early 1920's. It was a quiet rural area, thirty miles from New York City. Large tracts of land were available at very attractive prices. Zoning restriction appeared to be minimal or non existent. Immigrants, while not encouraged, were accepted in the area. The Stelton community besides being self governed had its own school, a very progressive school, The Rand School. The commute to Newark and New York City was longer and more expensive. To Somer's way of thinking, Chatham Township was his first choice. He envisioned a "Commuters Colony."

THE GATHERING OF THE FLOCK

WITH RENEWED VIGOR AND DETERMINATION Somer lost little time in implementing "phase two." Phase two was the gathering of his following to form an exploratory committee. He had kept records of those who indicated strong interest in his project. The list was transformed into "real people" with "real names." Sheib, Robbins, Thorner, Sachs, Chaffez, Greenberg, Deutch, Rubenchick, Stuckleman, Eisenscher, Honixfeld, Katz, Abbazia, Langer, Weiss, Coffet, Koukley, Rubin, Fogelson, Shipler, Gordon, Seaser, Blumen, Mollod and Lipschitz. These were the most actively recruited names in the early stages of the development. Somer contacted all those on his list of "interested" and arranged an organizational meeting at the Rand School, in New York City.

Somer quickly discovered the "recruits" were very diverse in their occupations and professions. The following is a list of the recruits and their occupations and their professions.

Lewis Thorner: Men's Tailor

Oreste Abbazia: Electrician, A veteran of World War 1, United States Army Air Force.

Frieda Abbazia: Seamstress in a "sweat shop," that made only black mourning dresses.

The Chibka's: Joe and Goldie were sample dress makers for Ceil Chapman, New York's most famous fashion designer.

Morris Langer: A furrier and then a Union organizer for the fur trade. Instrumental in Unionizing Hollander Furs in Newark, N.J. [Hollander Furs was one of the largest fur tanning companies in the world]

Ber Coffit: Sculptor

Bertha Robbins: Teacher, Taught Russian

Isreal Katz: An accomplished artist, painter, sculptor, and designer of expensive dishes.

George Koukley: Gifted base violin virtuoso with the New York Philharmonic Orchestra and the NBC Symphony Orchestra [Arturo Toscanini Conductor]

Max Weiss: Cloth cutter in a coat factory

Samual Gordon: Dentist, office in New York City.

Benjamin Sheib: Pioneered motion picture titles, best known for the titles for "News of the Day" shown between double features at movie theatres in the 1930's through the 1950's .

Ike Eisenscher: Bookbinder, Prudential Insurance Company, Newark, N.J.

Bernard Somer: Bookbinder, Prudential Insurance Company, Newark, N.J.

David Bernstein: Writer for a Jewish newspaper

Penoff: A carpenter, amateur violin player

Solomon Robbins: Editor of "The Forward"

Jacob Sachs: Optician

Harry Mollod: Owned and operated a very successful insurance agency on Church Street, New York City

Boliaslov Kondrat: Plumber

Nadia Kondrat: Practical Nurse and Author. All her writings were in Russian

Soloman Schipler: Carpenter

The first order of business was to give the new organization a name. They decided to call the organization The Chatham Colony Association. This seemed to be a fitting title because the potential site of their endeavor would be Chatham Township, New Jersey. The second order of business was to appoint a committee of five to affirm or reject Somer's selection for the new community.

The committee members were Chaffetz, Coffet, Deutch, Rubenchick and Sachs. The group made several Sunday afternoon trips to walk the land and gage the commuting time and distance to and from Chatham and New York City. They must have sensed the same emotions that gripped Somer. The entire committee enthusiastically concurred with Somer's choice for a site.

THE INTRODUCTION OF "UTOPIA" TO THE FLOCK

THE NEXT ORDER OF BUSINESS was to locate the Estes family. When researching the Township tax records, Somer's came upon the name of a Webster. C. Estes and his wife Jennie as the owners of the property. The entire Estes property was one hundred and forty five acres. Webster and Jennie were residing in Babylon, New York. Somer and the newly formed executive committee quickly established contact with Webster and Jennie Estes. The Estes family directed the committee to contact their attorney, Edward H. Lum Esquire. Edward H. Lum happened to be a prominent attorney in Chatham and Morris County. He was a member of the highly respected Lum family in Chatham. The contact with the Estes and Edward Lum intensified the efforts of Somer and the Executive committee to acquire the Estes property. Convinced that the long sought after "Utopia" had been discovered, Somer initiated a campaign to introduce the property to the newly organized members through the mail. The following is the letter sent out to the members.

THE MEETINGS BEGIN

LETTER DATED OCTOBER, 13^{TH,} 1921, New York

"At a meeting of the Chatham Colony in Mrs. Robins' [Robbins] home held on Wednesday, October 12th, 1921, it was decided that all those wishing to visit the site meet in Hoboken on Sunday, October 16th, 1921 at the Lackawanna R.R Terminal, 15 minutes before train time. Mr. Somer will meet you there.

                Are you in it?

Bring your friends and bring your lunch.

Trains leave Hoboken for Chatham, N.J at 9:45 A.M.

One way fare is 65 cents, from New York City.

Ferry leaves 15 minutes before trains at Barcley Street, Christopher Street and West 23rd Street. I am truly yours, B. Somer

            1517 Washington Avenue

            Bronx, N.Y.

THE BEGINNING OF NEGOCIATIONS

THIS EXCURSION TO THE PROPERTY prompted the following letter to Edward Lum.

Letter dated October 17th, 1921

Mr. Edward H. Lum, Esq.
Chatham, N.J.

My Dear Mr. Lum,

A committee of the purchasing organization was out in Chatham on October 16th, 1921 to look over the grounds and it so happens that this committee does not substantiate my report on the merits of this place. Only to a certain extent, here is what I am fully authorized to offer on their findings.

1] $150.00 per acre
2] $6,000.00 down
3] $100.00 on option till March 31st, 1922
The rest of your communication is satisfactory. Should I receive a favorable reply, I shall immediately proceed to draw up an agreement for your approval.
I am very truly yours, Bernard Somer

This poorly worded letter was sent in the very early stages of negotiations for the purchase of the property to all the members. It did solicit an instant reply from Mr. Lum. While Lum's reply did reject the seemingly inadequate, flimsy offer, Edward Lum in the same letter outlined the condition for the sale. Lum's reply prompted the following correspondence from Somer to the members. Somer's letter covered the items pertinent to the sale of the property. The following is the notice with all of its grammatical mistakes sent to all the members.

Notice dated October 19th, 1921

B. Somer
1517 Washington Avenue
Bronx, N.Y.C

Dear Friends,

I am advised by our friend Bertha Robbins of 111th Street, to communicate with you about a Colony that we are organizing in Chatham, N.J. The membership of this colony is limited to one hundred members, each one to settle on an acre.

The place we have in view is 24 miles from the City of New York, on the Lackawanna Railroad, 500 feet above the sea level, rolling country, good soil, electricity, 15 minute walk from the depot, wooded, commutation $10.54 per month, 29 trains a day at Chatham, N.J, one hour ride from N.Y. C.

There is 145 acres to be had and the owner wants $200 per acre, if bought in bulk.

On Sunday next, October 23rd/21, I am going out to show the place to all prospective members. Should you want to join us you could meet us at the Lackawanna R.R. terminal, Hoboken, N.J. on Sunday, next, Oct. 23rd

(9:45 A.M) nine forty five A.M. Bring a lunch, and bring your friends. In buying this place cooperatively, it will stand each member a pro rata share of what it will cost.

The following months saw the negotiations drag on with sporadic offers and counter-offers. During this period of impasse, Somer and the committee continued their efforts to recruit new members to the organization. The following is one typical recruiting letter.

Letter dated December 6, 1921.

Dear Friends and Comrade:

The enclosed paper is an outline of what the new Colony is set to accomplish. We therefore ask you to investigate our proposition by attending the next meeting of the Colony which will be held at 62 East 106th street, City, on Friday evening, December 9th, 1921, at 8:15 P.M. sharp.

As outlined, we aim to establish a commuters Colony near enough to the City to warrant building permanent homes for those who desire to do so. You will realize that time passes quickly and we would like to go out the coming spring. Some would like to camp next summer and be away from the City. To do this we must act and act quickly.

We have one place in view and it is the nearest so far, it is located in Chatham N.J. 24 miles form the City, on a main line of the Lackawanna R.R. 27 trains each way daily, passing through scenic country to Chatham N.J. 234 feet above the sea level. The owner wants 200 dollars per acre: he has 145 acres.

This place has electricity and telephone service to the property: the place is 20 minutes to the depot; 15 minutes from the trolley car; cement sidewalks for half the distance from the depot to the place. The Lackawanna terminal at Hoboken is adjacent to the Hudson Tubes which is a great asset for commuters.

A group of ninety or one hundred members could buy the whole tract up, each paying 100 dollars down; for the balance the owner will take the mortgage at 5%.

We want you to join, but first you must investigate, so do not forget our meeting place.

> I am truly yours,
> B. Somer, Organize

Letter dated January 12th, 1922

This "Dear friends and Comrade" letter reported on the actions taken at a special meeting held on December 15th, 1921. The following transpired, a motion was made and passed that an option be taken on the Chatham Township property for the purpose of establishing a commuters Colony and a Modern School. A committee of three, namely S. Robbins, B. Coffet and B. Somer were selected to implement the option. The committee will be ready to report and submit to the membership any proposition submitted by the owner of the 145 acre tract.

In anticipation of the owner's proposal, a special meeting was to be held Tuesday evening, January 17th, 1922 at 8:00 P.M. sharp at the H.S. Educational Center, 62 East 106th Street, N.Y.C. Room #3. Hopefully, final action will be taken for the purchase of the property. The letter, once again, described the qualities and attributes of Chatham and added two additional facts, "good black soil" and "a lake for bathing," ten minutes away. The new price for an acre is $172.00. The letter concluded with, "ALL THIS IS POSSITIVELY SO!"

> Hoping to see you at the meeting,
> I am sincerely yours,
> Bernard Somer

Letter dated January 26th, 1922

Florence Robbins, Secretary,
B. Somer, Organizer, 1515 Washington Ave.
Bronx, N.Y.

Dear Friend and Comrade,

The Chatham Colony Association will hold a very important meeting on Monday, January 30, 1922, at which meeting the very important question will be determined. DO WE GO OUT TO CHATHAM NEXT SPRING OR NOT?

NEGOTIATIONS INTENSIFY

THE 145 ACRES ARE OFFERED to us at present for $23,500.00. That is, $162.00 per acre. A real bargain! They agree to give us an option for $750.00 till May 1st, 1922.

We are at present 32 members in the association. Fourteen members have pledged at the last meeting the sum of $440.00 for the purpose of buying the option. How much money will you put up to buy the option?

If you are interested in a commuters Colony and a Modern School in the most picturesque place of the Jersey Mountains, we ask you to come to the meeting rain or shine and let us see where we stand. The meeting place is at 62nd East 106 St. in the Harlem Socialist Center Building. Our plan is that each member after the option is bought pay in $100.00 on each acre he or she subscribes to. A $100.00 payment by 100 families will cover the $10,000 deposit commitment.

For the balance we will raise a mortgage. Those members, who will pay in cash, will have the benefit of a 10% differential. We want this meeting to be a success both morally and financially. As soon as we get the option, we shall be able to strive and do greater things.

Hoping to see you at this meeting
I am sincerely yours,
B. Somer, Organizer

P.S. Bring your friends

Letter dated February 1st. 1922:

The meetings were now being called at a rapid pace. The letter of February 1st was called for the purpose of raising the balance of the $750.00 option money. As of Monday, January 30th, 1922, $40.00 plus $185.00 pledged at the meeting brought the total pledges to $625.00 toward the option.

It was decided to call the pledges on February 6th, 1922 at the meeting at the Robbins home. The members were given the option of mailing in their pledges to Somers's apartment at 1517 Washington Avenue, the Bronx.

Letter dated February 2nd, 1922:

The letter dated February 2nd, 1922 was mailed to all prospective members, detailing the latest Estes proposal. The proposal was as follows: purchase price, $23,500 for the entire 145 acres. A $750.00 non-refundable payment was due immediately to secure the option to buy the property. The option would expire on May 1, 1922. This latest proposal drew immediate interest and action from the membership.

Seventeen members quickly pledged $625.00 toward the option. This left a balance of $125.00. A meeting was called for Monday, February 6th, 1922 to be held at the Robbin's home, 1 East 111th Street, N.Y.C. for the purpose of calling in the pledges and raising the additional $125.00 to satisfy the option contingency. The letter also alerted prospective members and friends of the first organized excursion to Chatham on February 5th, 1922. Somer will personally meet and greet everyone between 9:00 and 9:30 A.M at the Barcley Street Ferry and conduct the tour to Chatham. The members and friends who accompanied Somer on that cold February day were excited, impressed, and in awe of what they saw and experienced. They were unanimous in their feelings. This was "Utopia!"

Letter dated March 2nd, 1922:

The committee was now in High Gear, with frequent meetings and intense negotiations with the Estes family. A letter dated March 2nd, 1922 announced adaption of a constitution and By-Laws. February 20th, 1922 had seen the executive committee agree to the terms of the purchase of the property. The terms, now in writing were Five Hundred Dollars, non-refundable, for a 120 day option. Ten Thousand Dollars was to be paid at the end of the 120 days. The Estes family agreed to hold a $13,000.00 mortgage at five per cent interest, for 36 months. To meet these terms each member had to pay in $105.00 spread over four payments. The good news letter alerted the members that the money for the option had been raised and better still 22 members out of the current membership of 40, had pledged $3,800 toward the $10,000.00 due in ninety days.

The members had the option to pledge-to purchase a holding. A holding was one acre of ground. They were given the option to purchase up to 3 holdings. Most members bought one holding, a few purchased two, while two members, Soloman and Bertha Robbins and Fannie and Louis Sachs pledged to purchase three. The holdings were in instant demand and quickly subscribed to.

PROGRESS

The next letter, dated March 9^{th,} 1922 addressed to "Dear Friends and Comrades" trumpeted the news that the Colony had satisfied the option to purchase the land as of March 6^{th,} 1922. The letter also detailed the committee's progress, plans and announcements for developing the property. The letter also announced that the Chatham Colony Association will be a cooperative society incorporated under the laws of the State of New Jersey and all fiduciary officers shall be bonded. The letter concluded with an invitation to all members and friends to join in a second excursion to the property on March 12th, 1922. The train fare will be 65 cents, round trip from Hoboken to Chatham. Somer, once again will be at the Barcley Street Ferry to lead the way.

The most interesting part of the letter was the proposed price of an acre of land. Each acre would be $162.00 and change. Applicants were required to put up $ 5.00 for each acre, he desires. The letter was signed B. Somer, Organizer.

Letter dated April 12th, 1922:

An optimistic executive committee had carried on a campaign to increase the membership and at this time felt they signed up the number of members necessary to continue with the project. Each new member had visited the site, subscribed, and paid in toward their holding. Notice of a meeting to be held, April 22nd, 1922 was sent in the next mail. The meeting will be held at the studio of Max Lipshutz, 93 Avenue B, corner 6th Avenue, N.Y.C.

Original members were to make their second payment of $25 per acre and new members were to make their first $25 per acre payment. A number of members suggested that an effort be made to collect the $10,000.00 deposit earlier than the June 15th, 1922 deadline. The desire to take possession of the land by many members was growing. Because of contractual deadlines the committee determined it would be necessary to hold weekly meetings.

The treasurer, Bertha Robbins, was placed under bond. The papers of incorporation were drawn up and recorded with the county office and sent to the Secretary of State in Trenton for his signature. The next membership meeting was to conduct the following business:

1, Payment of land
2, Report of Organizer
3, Adoption of constitution
4, Establishment of water and roads
5, New business

It was suggested that members bring anyone interested in joining the Colony to the next meeting and introduce them to the membership and the committee. A P.S, announced that Bertha Robbins, Secretary of the Modern School Association and Social Center will give a full report on its progress to locate in the Colony.

Notice of another excursion to the site on April 16th at 9:30 from the Barcley Street Ferry with Somer leading the way ended the letter. The price was still 65 cent round trip.

Undated letter, about April 15th, 1922:

The next meeting will be held on Saturday evening, April 22nd in the studio of Mr. Lipshutz, one of our members.

This will be a big opportunity for the members to get acquainted with each other as this is the first general meeting of the Colony.

The first members will make their second payment

The new members will make their first payment.

It was suggested by a number of members that the $10,000.00 be raised earlier than June 1, 1922. This would enable the association to take possession of the tract at an earlier date. The committee felt the suggestion should be made part of the order of business at a future meeting.

Address: 93 Avenue B, corner 6th. St. N.Y.C.

This letter was signed by the entire executive committee.

> B. Robbins
> B. Chaffets
> Dr. L. Sachs
> Harry Deutch
> B. Rubenchick
> B. Somer

Letter, Undated shortly after April, 22nd, 1922:

The letter detailed the progress of the meeting at the studio apartment of our friend, Max Lipshitz. The atmosphere at this meeting place, added to the good fellowship.

Somer gave an upbeat report on what had been accomplished in the past few weeks. First, a bank account had been opened with the State Bank's Fifth Avenue branch in the name of The Chatham Colony Association. Forty four members had subscribed to 67 acres in writing. The question of taking immediate possession of the land was discussed by the members present. Those in attendance enthusiastically pledged $7, 695 toward the $10,000. They voted to raise the balance of $3, 305 by Saturday evening May 6, 1922. An assessment of $1.75 per acre was voted on and passed to cover the cost of acquiring the Search and Title Guarantee documents. The letter also indicated a sense of urgency by announcing that all members be present on April 29th to enact very important business.

1. Payment of land and admission of new members.
2. Report of organizer
3. Adoption of constitution
4. Election of officers
5. New business

The April 29th meeting was fruitful. It was a success both morally and financially. First, new members were admitted with their down payment. The constitution was voted on and passed on the second reading. The financial report showed current subscriptions: $7,695.00 and new subscription of $1,255.00, making a total of $8,950.00 with more members to hear from. The last item of the letter noted that the Sunday excursion was a decided success. The letter was signed, I am fraternally yours, B. Somer

Letter dated May, 2nd, 1922:

The letter reflected the upbeat mood that had given encouragement to the committee because of the progress of the project since the last meeting.

A May 6th, Saturday night meeting would be held at the Lipshutz Studio, 93 Avenue B, N.Y.C. at 7:00 P.M sharp. The committee urged everyone to attend this "memorable event" in the life of the Colony.

The executive committee reminded everyone to bring with them their pledges of cash, money orders or checks. Any one of the three would be acceptable. The feeling of the committee was that with the pledges of the current members added to new member's pledges, the goal of $10,000.00 would be realized at the Saturday meeting. This meant that the Colonist would take title of the property and begin the implementation of the "Dream."

FRUSTRATION

The May, 6th meeting turned out to be a disappointment for Somer and the committee. It did not turnout to be the memorable event they had hoped for. The anticipated pledges were not forth-coming, leaving the committee still short of the $10,000 required deposit payment.

Undated letter sent about May 7th, 1922:

A special meeting was quickly called for May 13th at the Lipshutz studio. The purpose of the meeting was:

1. Payment for land
2. Final adoption of the constitution
3. Nomination and election of officers for the year beginning, May, 1922
The financial status to date was as follows:
Number of members-62
Acres subscribed for-68
Money pledged --- $8,368.80
Pledges in the bank ---$4,363.70
Pledges outstanding ---$4,005.10

The letter stressed the urgency of bringing in the balance of their pledges to "Get the Land". It was further reported that the Guarantee Title and Insurance Company from Passaic, New Jersey was to do the title search and the surveying of the property. The letter was signed:

Lillian Fine, Secretary

B. Somer, Organizer

Letter dated May 24th 1922:

The tone of the letter expressed concern, impatience and frustration with the membership's slow response in fulfilling their financial obligation to the association. A meeting on May 27th was held at the Lipshutz at 7:30 P.M sharp! Underlined in the letter was,

Special Order Of Business, Payment Of Land

Every member is, kindly asked to bring in the balance of his or her pledge, as we have received word from the Guarantee Title and Insurance Company that the deadline for the $10,000.00 was drawing near. This means "we must have the money!" Out of the $10,000.00 pledged, a balance of $3,442.50 remains outstanding. On the lighter side, notice of a picnic outing at the property was being planned in conjunction with the taking title to the property. It will be an all day affair with the committee providing soft drinks and ice cream. Members were to provide for their picnic lunch and were required to make reservations with the sight seeing touring cars. The cost of the trip would be determined later. The members at the meeting on May 13th voted that all organization expenses be divided equally among the membership. The amount of $4.00 was assessed each member.

The hastily arranged May 27th, meeting proved to be the long delayed and eagerly awaited "memorable event" meeting. The $10,000 deposit money was finally collected, in the bank and ready to be turned over to the Estes family, well before the June 15th deadline. The time had come to celebrate and begin the implementation of the Dream. The third phase of the project, securing the down payment for the land was now a reality. The final phase, taking title to the property was only months away!

The whirlwind pace and the deadlines ended suddenly. The June 17th meeting acted on the recommendation of the executive committee to hold meetings every two weeks instead of once a week. The executive committee felt that much of the important business could be transacted at executive meetings. A motion for the change was made and passed.

The executive committee now acting as a bill collector reminded everyone by letter that money still outstanding for assessments, dues or land, must be paid at the executive Committee Meeting, Tuesday, July 27th at the Comrade Robbin's home, 1E-111 ST. The next meeting will be held at Comrade Lipshutz's studio, Saturday, July 1st. 1922, signed L. Fine Secretary.

Letter dated July 26th, 1922:

This letter announced a change of the date and the meeting place. The new date, July 29th, 8:30 sharp, at the People's House, 7E, 15th St. Room 407. Besides conducting the usual Colony business, a Mr. Woods had been invited to talk about Colony Problems. There are no letters, documents or records to describe what the Colony Problems were. Signed L. Fine, Secretary

DELAY AND SUCCESS

NOTICE TO MEMBERS, AUGUST 17TH, 1922:

The notice announced that at the executive meeting held on August 8th, it was decided to postpone further membership meetings pending the clearance of the title.

The committee reported that an objection had been raised by the Guaranty Co. concerning the location of the Right of Way. The attorneys on both sides were diligently working to clear up the objection.

The committee announced that they meet every Tuesday night at the home of Mrs. Robbins. The notice, ended with the hope that "the next letter you receive will be to the effect that the title has been "CLOSED!" L. Fine, Secretary.

Letter dated September 7th, 1922.

The members were put on notice of a special meeting to be held September 9th, 8:00 at the Lipshutz Studio for the sole purpose of discussing the Consideration of Title. The Consideration of Title appeared to be the formality of putting in writing the specific terms of the sale namely, who, what, when, where and how. The original signed contract was still in force.

Letter dated October 25th, 1922

FINALLY, THE COLONY FOURTH OF JULY

The news that all the members were waiting for arrived in the mail. The letter trumpeted the news that the Chatham Colony Association had closed on the Estes property on October 19th, 1922. This date became the Colony's Fourth of July! The committee and the membership looked forward to the eagerly awaited celebration. No fireworks, rather, a dinner and a very pleasant program. All arrangements were left in the hands of the Chatham Modern School Association.

The next meeting will be held at the Lipshutz Studio, 8:00 P.M on October 28th. The important question of how to finance future improvements in the Colony will be the topic of discussion. The executive committee recommended that a monthly assessment of $10.00 toward improvements and a $5.00 monthly assessment toward the land. "On this question the members must decide as they will be the ones to pay".

Very truly yours, Lillian Fine Sec'

P.S. Your attention is called to the following sum still outstanding, $ _____ which must be paid at this meeting.

Letter dated November 15th, 1922

The next meeting will be on November 18th at the Rand School, 7 East 15th, St. N.Y.C. The first installment on the third assessment is due, also,

November's land payment. Members were reminded that all payments had to be prompt to meet new obligations. One such obligation was an invoice from the surveyor.

Lillian Fine, Sec'y.

SIGNS OF LOCAL DISCONTENT
FIRST SIGNS OFANTI-SEMITISM

THE MANY EXCURSIONS BY MEMBERS and prospective new members to the property did not go unnoticed by the residents of Chatham Township. Some residents became apprehensive and suspicious of the men and women who dressed differently, many wore a suit and a Fedora hat in their visits, spoke a different language and did not converse with the local residences. Rumors of the character, background and the motives of these "interlopers" found its way into daily conversations and concerns of the locals.

The Chatham Press on August 26th, 1922, had reported the following: "Delay" in finally taking title to the property has caused no end of rumors to go around, that the Association could not make a go of the scheme and would forfeit their deposit; that wealthy residents of the Township would take up the option at a profit to the Association, for the purpose of keeping them out. That the Association was "composed of the lowest type of Eastside Jews and that certain ruin to all real estate values was certain to follow their introduction to the Township." The Colony's image was that of a hot bed of radicals.

A small group of residents feared the new comers were, "a bunch of bomb throwing Communists." Talk of "throwing up armed road blocks" by some land owners adjacent to the property was another rumor at the time.

SOMER'S PRESS INTERVEIW

PART OF THE LENGTHY ARTICLE was Somer's answers to the reporter's pointed questions.

Question #, 1.   Why the delay in taking title?

Somer's answer: It is an old estate with many legacies, rights, and encumbrances, plus a paper right of way caused the delay. "We hope to have resolved quickly."

Question #, 2.   Character of the members?

Somer's answer: Commuter types, that included, doctors, lawyers, newspaper men, writers and mechanics, in fact, business and professional people entirely. Many of the members were mutual friends, thus assuring a congenial atmosphere. "Their plan was NOT to set themselves apart, but they would welcome their neighbors and cooperate in anything for the public good so far as their cooperation was desired and allowed."

Question #, 3.   What were their plans for a community?

Somer's answer: The plans included laying out the streets and the water lines. Individuals would build their own homes. Two of the projects planned were a community center and a private school. Somer was careful to explain, while these projects were planned, they were not part of the association's program. The association would donate the land but not undertake the construction of the buildings.

Somer's answers to the three most pressing questions seemed to have pacified the reporter and the readers of the Chatham Press for the time being.

The once a month, Saturday night meeting, became a significant part of the Associations members' lives. The meetings in the early stages of Colony development were held at various locations in New York City. The Harlem Club, People's House, and the Rand School all became the site of Colony meetings in the months after the acquisition of the land. The members focus was now directed toward the development of the basic staples namely good roads, reliable water supply, and a dependable source of electricity.

TAKING SHAPE

THE MEETINGS AT THIS TIME were focused on Colony business civil in nature and very lengthy. Three and four hour meetings became the norm. Somer, "The Organizer", was now the President of the Association. He spearheaded the road project. The first order of business was the hiring of a surveyor to lay out the individual plots. While this procedure is sometimes done prior to the closing, the committee waited until they took possession of the land before incurring any added expenses. They engaged the well known and reputable firm Arthur S. Pierson out of Morristown N.J.

The Colonists in their foresight dedicated a four acre tract at the corner of Spring Street and School Avenue for future development of cultural and recreational facilities. This one act of land dedication created a community within a community. Unwittingly the Colonists were establishing a blue print for future "planned community living." Consider this, they planned and developed their own roads, water system, Community center and recreational area. Looking back, the Colony was the prototype for many of today's adult communities.

1923/1924 – Unknown Helper, Penoff, Joseph Honixfeld preparing to "pull stumps."

With Somer's recommendation the Colony purchased a tractor. Early in the spring of 1923 the tractor was put to work in preparation for the road construction. The committee did engage a manager to oversee the road project. Members volunteered their time and skills in clearing the under brush, cutting down trees, and pulling stumps. "Stump pulling" became the Colonists week end past time. Joseph Honixfeld was the member entrusted with operating the tractor. He was assisted by Oreste Abbazia, Lorenzo Passanto, Penoff and Somer to name a few. Exhausting, back breaking, best described the work. For all those involved, it turned into a labor of love. The construction of the road continued well into 1923. The project became a true American Adventure.

The Colonists set aside the unsold property at the Southeast corner of Maple Street and School Avenue, now 9 School Ave. as a home for the tractor. They built a 10' by 15' wood frame, dirt floor shed. No plumbing, no electricity. The corner in the early 1930's became the social center for the teenage boys in the Colony. Warm summer nights found the boys hanging around the shed, talking about girls, a little politics, nothing in particular, and an occasional card game. With the introduction of electricity the corner street light kept the boys hanging around well after dark. Stuckelman, Weiss, Pomerantz, Gibson, Eisenscher, Barlus, Kondrat were the nucleus of this teenage boy's group.

THE ROADS

1923 – Arthur Pierson, Nathan Ceaser, Lillian Fine, Bernard Somer
laying out the future location of Maple Street.

THE ROADS WERE NOW DEFINING the shape of the Colony. The pre existing streets were Pine Street to the North, Lafayette Avenue to the East, Southern Boulevard to the South and to the West, acres of land owned by the well established and prominent Noe family. Situated in a ravine on this undeveloped property was a small pond, known to the locals as "Kelly's Pond." It was part of the Noe property that bordered on the westerly side of the Estes property. It was "The Rockefeller Center" skating rink for the young and old in the Township. The pond exists today at the end of Linden Lane.

Floral Street began at Lafayette Avenue and dead ended at Noe's undeveloped property. Noe's undeveloped property is now Rolling Hills, a million dollar sub division in Chatham Township. Spring Street commenced at Lafayette Avenue and ended at School Street. The intersection of School Avenue and Spring Street became the site of the original Colony Pool, presently known as the Colony Club. School Avenue was laid out to run parallel to Lafayette Avenue and connected to Maple Street, Floral Street and Spring Streets. The residential area of the Colony was approximately one square mile.

Chatham Colony Association Inc. Established October 19th, 1922

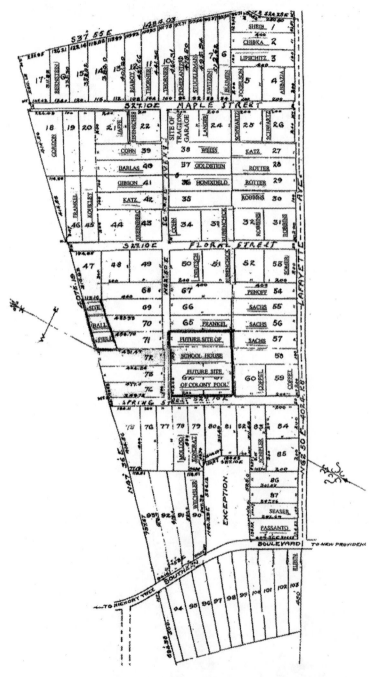

Colony Tax Map – Original Owners

WATER, PRECIOUS WATER

WATER WAS THE NEXT STEP in the development of the Colony. A public source of water was unavailable at this time for this new sub division. Research and inquires by the executive committee indicated a waiting period of three to five years or longer to install a public water supply for individual building plots. Minus any options the membership took on the task of creating their own source of water, a community well.

An engineering study found the lowest section of Spring Street, where it intersected with School Avenue was the ideal location for the well. There were several unsuccessful borings. Finally an artesian well, approximately 220' deep was sunk in the Spring Street plot adjacent to what would become the Colony Pool. A 10,000 gallon steel retention tank was buried in the ground near the pump house in the winter of 1924. The selection of this site turned out to be a "stroke of genius." Not only did the well supply water for every home, the well became the secondary source of water for the future Colony Pool! The primary source of water for the pool would be the many natural springs in the area. As of the year 2011 the original, 12' by 15', pump house still stands at the Spring Street location.

THE ORIGINAL PUMP HOUSE

Original Pump House. Operational 2011

VISABLE ACTIVITY

THE NEXT EIGHTEEN MONTHS, OCTOBER of 1922 to April of 1924 saw a flurry of activity and visible progress. A news letter in May of 1924 detailed the progress of the community water system. A temporary water line over 6100 feet in length had been installed above ground to provide water to the early Colonists. In addition to the roads and the water supply system, plans for the community house were on the drawing board.

The flurry of activity was creating an urgent need for electrical power to keep pace with the building boom. Jersey Central Power and Light recognizing a potentially large, lucrative customer base in the only new development in the Township accelerated the installation poles and wiring. The "precious juice" as described in the Colony News letter was made available to the early home builders.

Clearing for a baseball field was started on land that is now adjacent to the P.S.E.G high tension lines.

COMRADE

In reading the minutes of the meetings in the early 1920's and continuing into the 1940's and 50's, many Colonists addressed one another as Comrade at Colony meetings. The term Comrade was also used as a fraternal greeting for many members in every day greetings. Some members did use Comrade in its political sense, fellow Communist, to the people in the Colony. It was part of the vocabulary they brought with them from their European heritage.

The year of 1923 marked the arrival of the early pioneers in the Colony. Hyman Rubin and Joseph Honexfeld and their families, survived the winter of 1923/1924 in unfinished buildings.

THE BUILDING BOOM BEGINS

A "BUILDING BOOM" WAS STARTING. Rumor was that Louis Sachs, an optician, was starting the construction of a bungalow on 308 Lafayette Avenue which was to be completed by spring. Jacob Blumen was preparing to start construction of his bungalow on Maple Street. Somer was completing a garage. Rubin was now adding four chicken coops to his "estate." Yes, the building boom was started.

Colony's first newlyweds, Louis Thorner and Clara Morrison.

In other news, the first marriage in the Colony was about to take place. Louis Thorner and Clara Morrison were about to enter into the state of holy matrimony. The population of the Colony was about to increase. Three thousand five hundred, White Leghorn chicks will be arriving as "guests" at the chicken coops of Rubin and his business partner Joseph Schwartz.

THE COMMUNITY HOUSE

AND THE QUESTION, "DON'T YOU think it's about time to get busy on the "Community House" was put to the membership. They did get busy.

The Community House turned out to be a 20' by 20' wood frame structure. A 20' by 20' attached wooden platform led to the front door. The wooden platform served as a stage for formal summer activities, fund raisers, [United Jewish Appeal], concerts, speakers, political rallies and a platform for the younger set to enjoy games, such as four corners and tag. The title Community House and School House became synonymous. They were one and the same. The colonists never planted a tree, a shrub or a blade of grass at the community house, during its entire existence.

One room with a small storage closet took up the entire one story building. A wood /coal-burning pot stove was positioned against one wall. No one remembers being cold at winter meetings in the Community House.

No inside plumbing! One hundred feet into the woods, an unlit dirt path led to the bathroom accommodations, a two seat outhouse! For those who used the outhouse, an old Forwards newspaper, a Farmers Almanac or a Sears Roebuck Catalog were conveniently available.

1970's - Remodeled Community House.

CENTER OF ACTIVITIES

THE COMMUNITY HOUSE BECAME THE center for Colony business meetings, social functions and recreational activities. All the meetings were now held in the Community House. The Community House was "home" to social functions and recreational activity. A second hand player piano graced one wall. The song played most often was Chop Sticks and always as a duet. To this day the original Colony kids can only play the left hand or the right hand, but never both hands of Chop Sticks. The player piano came with one player roll, "Dardenella." Colony kids pumped out "Dardenella" as fast as their feet would go. It was played thousands of times, over the years.

Many of the members and their children saw their first Charlie Chaplin Movie in the Community House. The movies were silent films with captions. The first talkie, The Great Train Robbery, was still a few years from being filmed. Sara Schipler became the first and only official reader of the captions. No one remembers appointing or electing Sara to this position. But, Sara was articulate and dependable. Sara never missed a picture! A ping pong table was set up in the center of the room. Ping pong became the most popular indoor game in the Colony. It was the only game. The Colony kids played a lot of Ping Pong. Sol Horowitz was the perpetual champion.

Whether it was a Fourth of July party or a United Jewish Appeal fund raiser, all social events took place in the Community House. The most memorable event took place in 1937. The nephew of General Pershing, of World War 1 fame was the invited feature speaker at a fund raiser and recruiting rally in support of the Spanish Loyalists. The Loyalists were making what turned out to be a futile attempt to turn back the insurgent National Army led by General Fransisco Franco. The Colonists did raise money at this rally to support the Loyalists in their battle to defeat the insurgent, tyrannical Franco.

Besides raising money the rally inspired Milton White, a member's son, to enlist with the Loyalist Army. Milty fought with the Loyalists to the unsuccessful end of the Spanish Civil War. White did return safely home, an uncelebrated Colony hero.

The bon- fire rally was typical of many events that took place at the Community House. The menu for most events was local corn, watermelon, Campfire Marshmallows and Rottella's Soda. Rottella made the best Root Beer and Cream Soda. Alcohol, beer and wine were never part of Colony affairs.

Children and adults surround Bertha Robbins, and Dr. Sachs Back Row.
DECORATION DAY GATHERING 1926

COLONY MEETINGS

THE COLONY MEETINGS BECAME A monthly happening for the socially and politically minded members. The colonists grew to know about each other on different levels. They learned about each other's private lives. They got to know each other's character traits, each other's foibles and each other's reasons and agenda for being part of the Colony. Last but not least, they got to know one another's political views and to what degree they held these views. What they had discussed and debated in private conversations and small groups was now being discussed at Colony meetings.

While the Colony meetings did address and take care of Colony business, more and more time was taken up with bickering, personal agendas and POLITICS! The political debates revolved around the virtues of Socialism over Communism and Communism and Socialism over Fascism and Capitalism and how Capitalism could <u>never</u> solve the working man's problems. The theme was always a better world for the working man. For reasons, now long forgotten, Oreste Abbazia and Michael Best resorted to a fist fight during a meeting. After each side engaged a lawyer, the case was settled out of court.

The Community House/School House served the colonists in many ways. Over the years there were occasional classes offered for the arts and languages. Bertha Robbins conducted classes for those interested in learning Russian. Caesor Stea, Bertha Robbin's son-in-law, conducted art classes. The Community House never realized Somer's and the original prime mover's dream of a permanent full time school. The Community House has been expanded and renovated since the Township purchased the property in 1969.

Looking back, the Colonists were predominately Socialist and had a strong influence in the decorum and atmosphere at the Colony meetings. The Socialists felt the way to solve the world's problems was through patience and evolution, not revolution. Those who espoused the Communist philosophy seemed radical and impatient in correcting the world's ills. One member was a declared Trotskyite. Leon Trotsky, a Radical Communist, was instrumental in creating the Soviet Union and had been expelled from the Communist Party by Joseph Stalin. Trotsky's philosophy was "blow up the world and start over."

Over the years (1930's, 1940's and 1950's) Colonists did mellow in their political views. Many of the original members and organizers during the forty-seven year life span of the Colony did become Democrats, Republicans or Independents.

THE THREAT

The biggest threat to Colony solidarity, unity and the eventual dissolution came in the form of the evil their political dogma riled against, capitalism and money! In the ensuing years, the Colonists did benefit from three unexpected "wind falls."

THE FIRST WINDFALL

THE FIRST WIND FALL CAME in 1928 when Public Service Power and Light purchased a portion of Colony land. The swatch of land was in the westerly area of the Colony, between School Avenue and Noe's property. The acquisition created a diagonal strip of land, 225' in width that commenced at Pine Street, across Southern Boulevard and continued through the Great Swamp. When finalized, a total of approximately twenty two acres constituted the deal. The price paid by P.S.E & G was a whopping $58,000 dollars. All the twenty two owners of parcels affected by the sale were given the choice to "swap" for another unsold lot in the Colony or accept a monetary refund. Colony records indicate that all twenty two affected land owners did accept the land swap. It was the perfect deal. Public Service was happy and the Colonists were thrilled. Why?

First, Public Service's plan for a power line had taken a giant step forward. The high tension lines were constructed and put into service within the next few years. How did the Colonists benefit? The $58,000 realized from the sale of approximately 22 plus acres was a bonanza for the membership. In only six years, 1922 to 1928, the value of one acre increased by 1600%. To put it another way, their $162.00 an acre investment was now worth approximately $2,636 an acre. The surplus was put into the general fund. Looking back, there was a hint of capitalism in this land deal.

The sale of the property to P.S.E&G did not pass without some Colonists feeling that their president, Hyman Rubin in negotiating with P.S.E&G had received money under the table. No formal action was ever taken by the Colonists against Rubin. Rubin did move soon after.

THE WATER HARDSHIP

THE WELL AND THE UNCERTAIN water supply did become a constant, recurring hardship in the early years for the Colonists. Frozen pipes, breaking pipes and the occasional need for pump repair gave the residents and the executive committee grave concern. The disruption of the water service at times occurred without notice. Alerting the fellow residents of a "no water" emergency became the responsibility of any member who happened to be at home. The method of alerting the Colonists to the emergency was to knock on each neighbor's door. If time allowed the residents were advised to fill up as many pots of water and their bathtub. This hit or miss response to a water emergency proved to be unreliable and unworkable. Why they didn't use the telephone to alert the neighbors had a simple answer. Only one Colonist, Hyman Rubin, had telephone service. A young Isadore Blumen remembers a water truck delivering water to his home. They slowly but surely came to the realization that a volunteer Water Company was not the wave of their future. Both the old and the young in the Colony learned from this experience that the two things man can not live without are air and WATER.

The water problem weighed heavily on the minds of the executive committee after colonists experienced frequent periods of no water in the late 1920's. They grudgingly reached out and negotiated with the Commonwealth Water Company to take over the Colony water system. After what seemed an eternity, the Commonwealth Water Company in the 1930's purchased water rights to service the Colony. With keen foresight, the Colonists retained the ownership of the well and the pump house. The well and the pump house became the main source of water during the life of the Colony Pool. One sobering memory for those laying the original water lines was when the trench on Spring Street collapsed and partially buried Lorenzo Passanto. Quick acting members averted a tragedy by extricating Passanto before he sustained any serious injuries.

THE BOOM CONTINUES

Typical bungalow in the 1920's.

THE BUILDING BOOM CONTINUED INTO the 1930's. The land owners from New York City were anxious to start their new life in the Colony. While a few did build year round homes, a larger number built what would be considered summer bungalows. Some pitched a tent on a platform. A chicken coop boom was also under way. Many of the land owners built a chicken coop before they built their garage and in some instances, before they built their homes. Looking back, the Colonists were on the cutting edge of the chicken boom!

The typical bungalows were small, with two or three bedrooms, one bathroom connected to a septic tank or a cesspool, small dining room, small living room and a small kitchen. The absence of stringent building restrictions in the Township explained the sub-standard construction of many of the homes, no insulation, unfinished plastered walls, no central heating system. The building materials that were used would be in violation of today's building codes. Many of the families erected outhouses. Some of these outhouses were erected on a neighbor's vacant lot. Outdoor showers were popular with many of the summer crowd. Those who, vacationed in the Colony during the summer months enjoyed a Spartan life style. No phones, no heat, no air conditioning, no refrigerators, no microwave, no television, no stores, no traffic lights, no local Temple and just a few people owned a car. It was a no frills Garden of Eden.

HOME SERVICIES

EVENTUALLY THE COLONY DID ATTRACT home deliveries. Milk trucks were visible in the early morning hours every day of the week except Sundays. Schwartz Dairy {Southern Boulevard} and Noe Farm {Southern Boulevard and Noe Avenue} were the most prominent local dairies. Mister Anderson's two cow farm was located on Southern Boulevard across the street from Schwartz's dairy. Anderson never had a delivery service. His customers went to his home to buy milk. "Old Man" Anderson only sold raw milk. He never did join the pasteurization craze. In the spring, Anderson's cows grazed in fields lush with onion grass. Thus, spring time at the Anderson dairy meant onion flavored milk! It never did catch on. The three local dairies were just a fraction of a very competitive milk industry in the Colony and the Township. Most of the early morning traffic in the Colony was the fifteen different milk companies servicing their customers.

It is interesting to note that the Schwartz dairy is now the adjacent to Glenmere Estates. Noe farm is now Rolling Hills Estates. Both of these sub-divisions are now million dollar addresses.

The years of 1928/1929 saw the immergence of Dugan Brother's bakery in the Colony. Dugan Brothers provided a delivery service of quality bread, cake, coffee, peanut butter and mayonnaise. Dugan Brothers was famous for their tasty Butter Fruit Ring, Cherry Nut Favorites and the Lady Baltimore layer cake.

Their first mode of delivery was by horse and wagon. The horse and wagons were garaged in Madison, New Jersey. The original site is now the Stop and Shop super market on Main Street, Madison. The first Dugan driver out of the Madison branch and the driver that had the Colony route was Oreste {Harry} Abbazia. He happened to be Somer's brother- in-law and an original Colony member.

Dugan Brothers did get competition starting in the early 1930's. The Bond Bread Company started delivery in the area in a truck and gave the residence of the Colony and the Township an alternate choice of baked goods. By the mid 1930's both Bond and Dugan were delivering with trucks. The home deliveries remained profitable up until the super markets became part of the suburban landscape in the 1940's. Slowly the bread trucks disappeared.

The Colonists consumed a lot of produce. Even those who were not strict vegetarians consumed an inordinate amount of fruits and vegetables in their daily diet. Their love of vegetables was a lure to the produce peddlers in the area. The families had their choice of four vegetable vendors. They were Nick Campana from New Providence, Vito Mondelli from Berkeley Heights, and Harry Harootunian from Chatham Township. George Brindle, the fourth vegetable man, while, not a Colony member, did raise his family in the Colony. It was not unusual for the Colonists to patronize all four. An historical note: Harry Harootunian became the founder of Harry's General Store on Fairmount Avenue. Part of Harry's Store became a U.S Post Office annex. Harry and his wife, Mary, were prominent figures in the Township for many years. Sadly the produce peddlers suffered the same fate as the bread companies, falling victim to the super markets.

The refrigerator had not replaced the icebox in the early days of Colony life. The Muchmore Brothers operated a house to house ice delivery in the Colony three times a week. Harry and Billy sold the precious refrigeration by the block. A block of ice weighed about twenty five pounds and sold for 25 cents. Their biggest job was to keep the kids from chipping and stealing ice chips from the flat bed truck, while they were wedging the block of ice into ice boxes. The ice on the truck was covered by a canvas tarp to reduce the melting of the ice. The Frigidaire eventually spelled retirement for the Muchmore Brothers. Ice tongs became a collectors' item.

The fuel of choice for heating one's home was coal, which was replacing wood. There were no other choices. The central heating system was a coal furnace located in the cellar. The Colonists had a choice of two coal delivery companies, the Fitz Coal Company and Harry Peck. Fitz was an out of area, company, while Harry Peck lived on Longwood Avenue in the Township. Peck "hawked" a great deal, "eleven dollars a ton and five hundred pounds extrie." The five hundred pounds extrie did attract a lot of customers in the Colony.

Coal furnaces meant coal bins. A portion of every cellar became a coal bin. The bin was always located under a cellar window. The coal was shot through the cellar window, using a coal shoot. It was easy to know when a coal delivery was made. First, the strong odor of coal penetrated the entire house and secondly, coal dust filled the cellar. Removing the ashes of the burnt coal became an every day chore for a member of the household. The ashes had a very practical use. When spread on snow and ice covered driveways and walkways, they provided great traction for cars and people. The 1950's saw the beginning of oil burners replacing coal furnaces. Coal bins along with the basements were being transformed into recreation rooms by the 1950's.

If anyone in the Colony did not raise chickens, they had a choice of getting their eggs and chickens from Thorner, Somer, Eisenscher, Rueben and Scheib. They had an unlimited choice of poultry suppliers.

Another important ingredient in the life of the Colonists was the newspaper. Walter Henrich and his family operated the newspaper stand at the Chatham Railroad Station. Henrich found that a home delivery of newspapers in the Colony was profitable. The Colonists were avid readers.

The most widely read papers in the Colony were the Newark Evening News, The Call, The Forward, New York Times and The Daily Worker. Henrich only delivered the Newark Evening News and the New York Times. The Call, The Morning Freiheit, the Forward and the Daily Worker came in the mail. The Morning Freiheit was a Jewish newspaper affiliated with the Communist Party.

The Daily Worker circulation department tried to recruit two of the young boys in the Colony to deliver the "Sunday Worker." Their reward was a penny a paper and a free Young Pioneer uniform. The Young Pioneers were the equivalent of the Boy Scouts of America, but with a Communist indoctrination. Jerry Beauclerk and Bert Abbazia the potential recruits turned down their very attractive offer. The Sunday Worker was never delivered by any of the Colony boys.

An unexpected service for the Colonists and their children was provided by Jenny Stuckelman. Jenny became the shoulder to lean on for both the young and the old in the Colony who had a problem or needed counseling. She was the neighborhood spiritual leader and psychologist. The Stuckelman door was always open to those in need of her gift of caring and sharing. The Community House was not the only site for Colony functions. Jenny Stuckelman opened her home on Maple Street to the younger Colony children in the mid 1930's and conducted classes in Hebrew and Hebrew songs. Her well- meaning endeavor had a short life span as the number of pupils decreased in a relatively short time and the classes were discontinued. Jenny was the Colony problem solver. Jenny and her teachings are remembered with affection by her former students and their parents.

Last, but not least, Mel Roasch, a kosher butcher from Orange, New Jersey made weekly Saturday night deliveries of kosher meats. Mel Roasch was a Saturday regular for many years. He made his deliveries after the closing hour of his butcher store in Orange, N.J. Thus, the Colonists found a way to survive getting many of their basic food needs without going to stores.

CAR POOLING AND SHOPPING

THOSE WHO FOUND THE NEED to shop at a store carpooled and drove into Summit to take advantage of the stores staying open until 9:00 PM on Friday nights. Summit became one of the first New Jersey towns to have a super market. The Bildner family of Summit, N.J. opened the first King's Super Market on Springfield Avenue in downtown Summit. King's Market grew into a chain of Super Markets over the years and to this day is a very successful high end chain of super markets. Bernstein's drug store was a Friday night "must stop" for families. Bernstein's will always be remembered for its pyramid shaped ice cream cones.

Very few, if any, of the women in the Colony ever learned to drive a car. In addition, many of the Colonists did not own a car. The Tyrone family from the Boro provided the only public transportation, Tyrone's Cab service. Tyrone's cab fare was about $1.00 for Colonists to get a trip by cab to Chatham.

The most valuable service for the younger Colony boys was the mechanical skills of Bobby Brindle, a teenager. Bobby was an expert at bicycle repairs and retro-fitting the steering mechanism of sleds. From repairing flat tires to replacing broken spokes, Bobby was a master. For three dollars he would convert a fixed front end sled {non-steering sled} into a steering sled. This talent was a stepping stone to his career as a master automobile mechanic.

Oh yes, there was a periodic traveling knife sharpening service!

FREE ENTERPRISE IN THE "RED ZONE"

WHILE MOST PEOPLE IN THE Colony did espouse Socialism and Communism there was an attempt by some to venture into the world of free enterprise. The first attempt took the form of a general store, a very small general store. The year was 1928 when Frieda Abbazia turned her 10' by 12' living room and the 8' by 12' sun parlor into the two room general store. The store sold milk, bread, cigarettes, canned goods, groceries and stove black. The store at 208, now 252 Lafayette Avenue, did a modest business for a few years. Unfortunately for Frieda Abbazia most of the modest business was on the books. Some of the sales turned into the barter system. One memorable barter deal was with Isreal Katz. Katz was an exceptionally gifted portrait artist. To make ends meet during the Great Depression Katz painted the gold leaf on very expensive China. This China became the method of exchange between Katz and Abbazia for groceries. The China dishes are still treasured by Frieda Abbazia's children to this day.

She also experienced inventory shrinkage also known as shop lifting. One case of shop lifting was brought to her attention by her eldest son Milton. It seems Milton, age nine, pulled a pack of unpaid for cigarettes out of the pocket of a teen age customer as he was going out the front door and asked the youth, "Where are you going with the cigarettes?" It wasn't long after, in 1933, the two rooms were converted back to a living room and a sun parlor.

Joseph Honixfeld turned his acre of ground at what is now 21 School Avenue into a small sand quarry and a junk yard. The Colonists over the years prevailed in closing down the junk yard. Honixfeld and the junk yard disappeared at the same time.

Original Samovar Tea Room – 54 Floral Street.

Original Samovar Sign.

The last attempt at entrepreneurship by a Colony member was made by a Mrs. Ida Koukley in the late 1930s and early 1940s. Mrs. Koukley converted her large living room into to a Russian Tea Room which she named "The Samovar." The tea room was located at 54 Floral Street adjacent to the high tension line. While the Colonists and the people from the surrounding area did enjoy the fine tea and fine coffee, cookies and crackers, the Samovar "fad" faded in the 1940's.

Many of the services that are basic to man's existence in the 2000's were never part of Colony living. The vast majority never paid for cutting or fertilizing a lawn, cleaning a gutter, hiring a cleaning woman, a carpet cleaning service, a phone bill, a window washer, or a dry cleaner. No one paid for maintaining a sprinkler system, a cable bill, a home security system, a smoke detector system, or a company to service a central air conditioning unit. Many of the women never saw the inside of a beauty parlor or nail salon.

STAUSS AND THE "GOVERNOR"

THE ONE SERVICE MOST COLONISTS did take advantage of was provided by John Stauss from Pine Street. Stauss and his horse, Frank, every spring plowed many of the fields that the Colonists turned into vegetable gardens. As close as he was to Frank, Stauss was closer to his long time, faithful, black helper. The only name anyone knew of this respectful, congenial, hard working man was "Governor." It was assumed that "Governor" roomed in the barn above the stable. Stauss charged $5.00 to plow a half acre field.

Frank was the source of additional income for Srauss. In addition to plowing the gardens each year, Stauss sold the Colonists horse manure for their gardens. While there was an abundance of chicken manure available to the gardeners, they found that chicken manure burned the foliage of the vegetable plants and eventually killed the plants. They discovered that Frank's excrement was the best fertilizer. The young boys were routinely eating from gardens week days while the week end owners were working. They avoided one garden when they quickly realized the fertilizer around one Colonists very healthy plants was not horse manure but rather human feces. The owner and his family were defecating in their own garden. The identity of this garden shall remain the boy's secret. The plowing service lasted 20 years and ended with the death of Frank.

The luxury of having a garbage collection service was optional. Most of the Colony members did not take advantage of either of the two scavenger companies, Carlone and Sons from River Road, Chatham Borough or Ellicks and Sons located on Southern Boulevard, the Township. Rumors of a physical confrontation between the two families to gain control of garbage business spread through the Borough and the Township at the time. Their rumored skirmish might have been the forerunner of big city garbage wars that were to follow.

The Colonists disposed of all the wet garbage, such as melon rinds, tomato scraps, cucumber peelings and fruit residue in a shallow pit away from their house or on a neighbor's vacant lot. In July and August it was not unusual to find small, healthy vegetable gardens sprouting from these garbage pits. The dry garbage was burned in a field. Plastic was not a recycling concern as plastic had not been invented. Recycling was still decades away.

The early Colonists, 1920's and 1930's, had two choices of disposing of waste, the septic tank or a cesspool. Most had a septic tank system. The periodical pumping out and emptying of the tanks was taken care of by Carl Gulick out of Whippany N.J. Gulick's clean out service was needed every two or three years. Gulick prospered until the Township and many of the neighboring towns installed public sewers in the late 1930's and continuing into the 1940's and 1950's. Those in the Colony who felt the need of a second toilet, built their own outhouse discreetly hidden by shrubs or trees or, once again in some cases on a neighbor's vacant lot.

TALKING TO THE "ENEMY"

JOHN STAUSS WAS A HARD drinking, "Goose Stepping" German immigrant who openly discussed politics with Colony members. The discussions centered on the positive effect a young German house painter named Adolph Hitler and his movement, Fascism, would have on the world. Naturally the Colonist's thinking was more in line with the doctrine of a recently deceased Russian by the name of Vladimer Lenin. This very hot topic in the 1930s, Communism versus Nazism, did not diminish the ability of each side to get along with one another. The Colonists got along with Stauss and other Nazi sympathizers in the Township over many years. The emergence of Adolf Hitler in the early 1930s saw some of the boys from the Green Village/ Britten Road section of the Township goose stepping down the halls of the Southern Boulevard School extending their right arm in a Heil Hitler salute. All the open, national feelings about the virtues of Communism and Fascism on both sides disappeared with the onset of World War 11.

Those Colonists who became U.S citizens did exercise their right to vote. In the 1920's, the Colonists had their choice of two Socialist Party candidates, Eugene Debs and Norman Thomas. Debs and Thomas did share much of the Colonists loyalty in the 1928 presidential election. Norman Thomas the perennial Socialist presidential candidate did receive the support of most Colonists. With the advent of FDR, Franklin Delano Roosevelt and the New Deal in 1932, the majority supported FDR.

Winters in the early days of the Colony were long and harsh. Outside of the infrequent movies at the Community House and the monthly Colony meetings the year-round residents seemed to be in hibernation. This was in sharp contrast to the activity in June, July and right up to Labor Day.

THE CREATION OF THE POOL

1933 – The Colony Pool.

THE YEAR 1928 SAW THE dredging and construction of what would become the center activity for both the young and the old Colonists. A one acre piece of swampy land was carved out at the corner of Spring Street and School Avenue. The Colonists quickly realize that the muck dredged from the site was a hidden "treasure" that had two unforeseen qualities and value. The first quality was, it made for unbelievable top soil for their gardens. Secondly, the muck became the cure all for a fever to a bee sting and from a bruise to a headache. This newly discovered natural resource became a source of revenue to the association. They sold the muck! And the children of the Colony, to this day, have never forgotten the healing power of Colony muck. It had the same impact as the introduction of Penicillin to the world.

A four acre parcel of land was fenced in so as to form the pool grounds. The bathroom facility happened to be the same two seat out house that serviced the Community house. The out house was not convenient for the bathers. The trip was an uphill climb and one hundred <u>yards</u> away. This fell into the category of very poor planning. The bathhouse was a wooden structure 10' by 20' petitioned off into three stalls. The girl's dressing stall was nearest the entrance door followed by a storage room stall and a boy's dressing room. It did not take long for an unplanned feature in the bath house to be discovered. A small hole had been gouged in the wall of the storage room that became a look-in to the girls changing room. It was a matter of a few days when the hole was covered over and never appeared again. On occasion the bath house became a meeting room for the younger boys. It was a fact's of life classroom for some of the uneducated boys. Many for the first time would learn the differences between girls and boys.

The pool was an instant hit. A concrete wall 165' long formed the deep end of the pool. The remaining three sides were left in their natural state, mud. Mud banks lined with cat tails, swamp grass and unidentified weeds completed a horse shoe shaped mud hole. The bottom of the pool consisted of the slickest, slimiest mud in the Township and the visibility under water was about 12 inches on a clear day. But it was great! The Colonists liked to think of it as a natural bottom pond.

The pool provided a diversity of things to do. Besides the unorganized diving and swimming competition there was one horse shoe pit with a set of unmatched horse shoes. Most of the kids became pretty good horse shoe players. The pool became a home to fish, turtles, frogs and snakes and, oh yes, one snapping turtle. Kids fished for catfish and sunnies. They learned to hold the fish eggs and the frog eggs in their hands and loved the feel of the slimy eggs, Colony Caviar, slipping through their fingers. They watched as the eggs turned into minnows and then fish. They couldn't believe the transformation of the frog eggs into pollywogs and then into frogs, sometimes a bull frog. The pool became a class in Marine Biology 101.

Catching a water turtle in the murky pool was impossible. On the other hand, catching bullfrogs was not only fun but became profitable. One member, Stan Wechsler, loved frog legs. The going rate for good sized bull frog legs was $1.00 a dozen. Wechsler bought and consumed frog legs as fast as the boys could catch them. Wechsler was one, large, happy man and so were the boys who supplied the frogs.

The boys entertained and mystified their Township friends with the "Sol Horowitz can stay under water seven minutes" illusion. Horowitz would submerge in the middle of the pool and swim underwater to the dense weeds and cattails at the corner of the concrete wall, completely out of sight. The Colony boys in unison took up the count as Sol remained hidden. After at least six or seven minutes, Sol would swim under water and resurface in the middle of the pool to wild cheering. He became a Colony legend.

The adults found the pool and the murky water to be very therapeutic. It was a familiar site to see Dr. Sachs, the Schiplers and other senior members at mid morning, standing in water up to their waist. The ritual was always the same. They would gently dunk themselves up and down while splashing water over their upper body and chanting the phrase, "L'chaim, L'chaim." The English translation of L'cheim is "Good Health."

Another local pool hero to the Colony boys was William "Max," "Valutch," Kondrat. Valutch was the everything water champion. Besides being the biggest guy, six feet two, 230 pounds, he set unofficial pool records for swimming the furthest, (over 3 miles), swimming over 65 yards under water, (over half the length of a foot ball field) and staying under water consistently for over two and a half to three minutes. This Colony pool training prepared Valutch for his two hour and fifteen minute battle of survival in the Niagara River Gorge.

On July 17, 1933 William Kondrat became the only person in history to survive the rapids and the two whirlpools without a floatation device. On August 18, 1933 Kondrat received a hero's welcome at the bus stop in the center of Chatham. To this day, in 2011, no one has duplicated his super human feat. The Colony hero became the accidental hero\ of the Niagara River Gorge. The published story of William Valarian Kondrat's odyssey can be found in the book "Niagara Rapid Transit, A One Way Ride," written by Bert Abbazia.

FAVORITE PASTIME

THE YELL BALL GAME WAS heard most Sunday afternoons during the summer months in the Colony, as the young men and boys walked down School Avenue to the Colony field. The ball field was the by-product of the Public Service land deal. The field was about 140' by 250' and was nestled between the Public Service High Tension Lines and the Noe property on the Westerly side of the Colony.

Noe's dense woods created the short 140' right field foul line. The Colony boys established the automatic ground rule double for any ball that reached the right field woods. The original ball field is now part of the tennis courts located under the high tension lines on School Avenue. Looking back, those Sunday afternoon softball games did develop a few good baseball players. Some went on to play for Coach John Fries at Chatham High School. Irv Weiss, Bert Abbazia and Murray Best come to mind.

Everyone who showed up played, even Lew Cohn. Lew had one artificial leg as a result of an accident at the Chatham train station in the summer of 1933. Lew was 22 years old. In rushing to board the Lackawanna train to Hoboken, he slipped under the train and lost a leg. After a long recuperation and with the use of an artificial leg, Lew became a valuable member of the Sunday afternoon ball games. Lew was a great hitter and could still play first base, but he did need a designated runner. His permanent designated runners were 10 year old Alex Koukley and six year old Bertie Abbazia. The Cohn- Koukley- Abbazia combo continued all through Lew Cohn's playing days. About four summers or when "Bertie" became Bert and Alex Koukley out-grew the role of a designated runner.

The 1930's were the height of the depression years. The adults found entertainment in having a neighbor in for tea and crackers and discussing their children, the schools and politics. Some of the Colonists attended their Union meetings. Those in the garment industry attended I.W.O {International Workers Order} meetings. The I.W.O was considered a radical group and would later be the subject of a trial in a New York Court. The outcome of these proceedings was the dissolution of the International Workers Union by the New York State Insurance Commission for political reasons. Many lawyers and scholars felt the ruling was a travesty of justice.

WINTER ACTIVITIES

THE POOL IN THE WINTER was home ice for the Colony kids, who took up skating. They did have a choice of three other sites: Diefenthalers on Lafayette Avenue, Noe's pond and Kelley's Pond. Choosing where to skate was determined by the thickness of the ice. Kelly's Pond was the first to freeze and the Colony Pool was the last. Diefenthaler's Pond was very small and was only used when three or four skaters showed up. Noe's pond was used on special occasions, because of the long walk for the Colony boys. There was a fourth seldom used site. It was the miles of low wetlands between Chatham Borough and Florham Park. When the infrequent combination of flooding rains and freezing winter temperatures collided they created the largest, most scenic outdoor skating rink in any of the surrounding counties. It still exists today and old timers still refer to it as the Freshet. It was a special experience for skaters.

While the activities of the older Colony Members were limited, the sons of the Colonists enjoyed many activities. Most of these activities were unorganized, unsupervised and required no equipment. Baseball and touch football were the only team games enjoyed by the boys. Because of the absences of any hard top areas in the Colony, basketball was not a team game for Colony boys. No one had a paved driveway until after World War II. Marbles games appeared about the same time the robins appeared in the spring. All the boys grew up playing outdoor games: Four Corners, Tag, Ringo Leveeo, Mumbledy Peg, Red Rover, Hide and Seek, Caddy, Marbles and games that the boys improvised.

Board games were part of growing up in the Colony. Checkers and chess were popular both indoors and outdoors for many of the youth. Card games did not attract most of the boys.

MOVIE INCENTIVES

THE STRAND THEATRE IN SUMMIT, now a mini mall, in the 1920's and 1930's followed Hollywood's trend in increasing attendance at movie theatres. The motion picture industry introduced the 12 and 15 chapter serial movie shorts. These 15 minute shorts were shown between the Saturday matinee double features for 12 or 15 weeks. Buster Crabbe starred in the 15 chapter "Tarzan the Fearless," Bela Lugosi was the lead in the 12 chapter "The Return of Chandu" and John Wayne had his first successful movie role in the 12 chapter "The Hurricane Express" serial. These were just three of many serial movies at that time. Many Colony boys religiously attended every chapter of these action, suspense filled shorts. Every 15 minute chapter ended with a cliff hanger situation. Whether it was a helpless young lady tied to a railroad track and about to be the victim of a speeding steam engine or the hero trapped in a tunnel about to be overwhelmed in a torrent of raging water, each chapter ended in a death-defying situation. Next Saturday could never come soon enough for the boys.

Adults were lured to the Strand movies on Tuesday nights by an assortment of giveaways. The assortment included knives, dishes and the "World Book of Knowledge". Each patron received one knife or one dish or one Book of Knowledge each Tuesday night. To receive a complete set of each giveaway the adults faithfully attended many Tuesday night movies.

SHOWTIME

Kneeling: Leo Chibka, Marty Carlin, Bernie Mollod, Gabe Katz.
Standing: Sylvia, Beatrice Katz, Judy Greenberg, Easter Thorner, Alex Koukley,
Nuncie Barlus, Camp Counselor, name unkown, Jerry Beauclerk off to right.

SUMMER TIME WAS SHOW TIME at the pool and the Community House.
Whether it was Shelly Rosen demonstrating the latest dance (the Shag) or
the twins, Morris and Alex, playing a harmonica duet, the entertainment
never stopped. The fact that both Alex and Morris resembled a young
Uncle Fester of the Adams's Family added to the entertainment. Shoeless,

shorts only, and first name only, Dave, was a scalp reader. He was able to measure intelligence by the location of bumps on one's head. Some in the group, including the girls, learned to read palms. Everyone was happy to find out they had a long life line. Larry (first name only) awed every one with his ability to do a back flip from a standing position. William Valutch Kondrat, two or three times each summer, would gather his admirers to watch as he bounced on the end of the diving board until the board cracked. The crowed joined in counting the bounces until they heard the sound of the board snapping. He loved audience participation. Ralph Rueter entertained the gang by swallowing worms for 5 cents a worm. He made 10 cents one summer. Sol Horowitz never stopped trying to improve his own personal best for swimming under water. Judy Greenberg in a two piece bathing suit was a head turner and a crowd pleaser. All she had to do is show up at the pool. Many out of the area young men drove by the Colony Pool just to get a glimpse of Judy. The Weisgerber family had a situation that the kids in the Colony thought of as being very humorous. At age six and nine Bobby and Billy Weisgerber had an uncle who they always addressed, with respect, as "Uncle Artie." It just so happened that their "Uncle Artie" was only four years old at this time. Looking back, it is still very amusing. Doctor Louis Sachs, the optician, became a Colony legend to both the old and the young after he demonstrated he could stick his own toe in his mouth. He had this gift until he was in his eighties! A very young Gabe Katz demonstrated his artistic talent by creating amazing life like replicas of nude females. Gabe displayed his talent on beech tree trunks, sandy beaches at the shore and a muddy bank at the Colony pool. Life was great for all those who were exposed to the Colony's summer activities.

TRAGEDY

WHILE THE COLONY SEEMED TO be a safe haven for its members and their families, life did present the Colonists with their share of sadness, tragedy, grief, and sobering moments. Tragedy did strike in 1933.

It was about 7:30/7:45 A.M on March 23rd, 1933 that a thunderous blast rocked everyone in the Colony and the surrounding neighborhoods. The vibrations from the blast were both immediate and long-lasting. The victim of this horrendous, cowardly act was Morris Langer. Morris Langer, his wife Ida and his two daughters, Ruth and Florence lived at 7 Maple Street. Little did the Colonists realize at that moment the notorious Murder Incorporated just paid an overnight visit to the Colony. During the night, at about 1:30 AM, a bomb was wired to the starter of Langer's garaged car by a professional hit man. The time was established by the barking of a neighbor's dog.

Children on their way to school that morning were jarred by the sight of the gapping hole in the garage roof. Some of the neighbors rushed to the Langer home and quickly realized the extent of his injuries. Langer's legs bore the brunt of the blast. One of the first neighbors at the scene was Rae Weiss. Rae happened to be one of the few women in the Colony who could drive a car. Rae drove Langer and his wife, Ida, to Overlook Hospital where Langer went through long, extensive surgery to save his life. Langer succumbed to his injuries four days later on March 27th, 1933.

All the Colony members and their children were invited to a memorial service that was held in the Community House, where a ten inch by fifteen inch, bronze plaque, was unveiled commemorating the tragedy. The plaque gave the date, time and circumstances surrounding Langer's death. Colonists young and old were shocked by what they read and saw. The plaque, adorned by a HAMMER AND SICKLE described his death as "assassinated because of his activity in the labor movement." Above the plaque, was a picture of Langer, lying on a table, with a cloth covering his body from his thighs to his bared shoulders. The photo revealed the lower part of his body was minus one leg. While the plaque and the picture were eventually mysteriously removed from the Community House, the memory of the plaque and the picture has never been removed from the minds of those who viewed them.

The assassination was the result of Langer's very vocal and active efforts to unionize the Hollander Fur Company in Newark N.J. In February, 1933 a conference meeting between representatives of the Needle Trade Workers Industrial Union and the Protective Fur Dressers Corporation was convened. On this night, Morris Langer spoke up very strongly against the Murder Incorporated controlled Protective Fur Dressers Union. For the next month Langer received and ignored numerous death threats. Two of the principals of Murder Incorporated, Louis "Lepke" Buchalter and Jacob "Gurrah" Shapiro allegedly assigned Jacob Shulman, a bomb expert, to muzzle Langer! The ASSIGNMENT was completed at 1:30 A.M on March 23rd, 1933.

Jacob Shulman, his wife and son happened to be short-term boarders at Sam Greenberg's home on School Avenue. For unknown reasons the the Colonists immediately suspected Shulman as the "hit man." Shulman's four year old son, Sandy, was subjected to the question, "Why did your father blow up Langer?" Five year old Bertie Abbazia remembers vividly asking Sandy this question. Jacob Shulman was never tried for Morris Langer's murder! The Shulmans moved to Newark N.J. Sandy, years later, does recall the night the men escorted his father out of their apartment. Sandy never saw his father again. It seems mob justice did prevail. Shulman's dismembered body was found in the Watchung Reservation in 1938.

It must be noted that Langer was not a stranger to the law. Langer's unionizing activities at the Hollander Fur Company in the 1930's made him well known to the Newark police department. Langer had been cited for illegal picketing and rabblerousing speeches on several occasions.

The Langer's connection to the Colony had a positive ending with the sale of their home and more specifically, the family that bought the house. William and Reesa Beauclerk and their daughter Dorothy, age 10 and their son Gerald age 6 purchased the home shortly after the ill fated event of March 23rd, 1933. Bill worked for a major bakery in Newark N.J as an engineer of equipment maintenance and equipment development. Beauclerk is credited with assisting in developing the first bread slicing machine.

Dorothy could be heard on Saturday mornings singing along to the music of the popular radio program "Let's Pretend." Jerry on his first day in Ms. Belcher's first grade class brought a bag of cherries to share and break the ice with his new friends. Jerry from that day forward was always referred to as "Cherries." "Cherries" will be remembered for two things, first for rescuing his faithful dog, Pete, from drowning in the Beauclerks outhouse and secondly as one Chatham High's greatest soccer goalies. He was in the net during the 1943 undefeated season and gave up only 5 goals all year! The Beauclerks became an integral part of Colony life for many years.

The second tragedy befell the Brindle family. George Brindle, his wife and six children Bill, Eddie, Mildred, Gloria, Bobby, and Georgie, while not Colony members, did rent a house on Maple Street. George Brindle, senior, sold fresh vegetables from his truck to the Colonists and residents of the Township. He managed to eke out a modest living. Opportunity came knocking on the Brindle door in the form of a job offer. He was offered steady employment as a bull dozer operator. Sadly on his first day at work in the Long Hill section of the Township, the bull dozer flipped over and crushed George Brindle. The entire Colony mourned Brindle's death. Mrs. Brindle never remarried and raised her six children to become productive citizens.

The word polio became part of the Colonists conversation in the 1930s. Suddenly in the month of August in the early 1930's Eddie Brindle fell victim to a crippling condition called polio. The prognosis for a polio victim was life in an iron lung. One suspected source of the polio virus was swimming pools. The month of August in the Colony was labeled as polio month. For the next few years families avoided swimming at the pool during the month of August. The polio scare subsided after a period of time that lasted a few years. The pool was once again the center of life in the Colony in June, July and yes, August. Eddie Brindle did recover from his bout with polio. Eddie went on to marry and raise a family. Polio awareness was part of the education for Colony kids.

The Lew Cohn story went from a debilitating near fatal accident to a truly inspirational story. Lew was the adopted son of the Rubenchicks on Floral Avenue. Life was good for this strapping, bright, energetic young student. It was on a warm summer morning, the year 1933. Lew was late getting to the Chatham railroad station for his daily commute to Cooper Union College in New York City. With the train in motion, Lew in his attempt to board the train, slipped and landed on the ground. Lew's right leg was crushed under the wheel of the train. He went on to become an osteopath, marry and have four sons, two of whom are doctors and two dentists.

It was in the early 1930's that the Frankel family on School Avenue was awakened to the smell of smoke. They quickly realized that their home was on fire. The damage was extensive. The Frankels and their son, Howie, were forced to find temporary housing outside of the Colony during the restoration of the home. The rebuilt home was a big improvement over the old home.

The Year was 1942. Norfolk Navel Base was the scene of the fifth tragedy to strike a Colony family. Joe and Jenny Stuckelman's heart must have stopped when they answered the knock at their front door. Two United States Navy Sailors stood at the door with an envelope. Their worst fears were about to be confirmed. Their son, Charlie, had been shot and killed in Norfolk, Virginia while on liberty and off the base. The circumstances of the shooting remain a mystery to the Colonists to this day. Charlie will be remembered as a tough young man and one of Chatham High Schools greatest soccer goalies.

Although the Weisgerber family from Longwood Avenue were not Colony members, the death of their son Eddie Weisgerber on D Day June 6th, 1944, had a lasting and powerful, emotional effect on the Colonists and his boyhood friends. Eddie was part of the first wave of allied troops to hit the beaches at the invasion of Normandy, France. Many of his Colony boyhood friends have not forgotten the gangly, farm boy, turned hero.

Each sad, tragic, horrendous event not only left its mark on every immediate family member but established a bond among the old and young residents of the Colony. Human qualities, charity and compassion towards one's neighbor became more evident with each tragic event. The Colonists, individually and as a group always helped anyone in need. The following story is an example of these qualities.

HEART WARMING

THE HEART WARMING STORY OF Cecilia Horiwitz, a sickly, unemployed, single mother raising her one son, Sol, comes to mind. Cecilia and Sol's involvement with the Colony began in the late 1920's. It was the depression years when Cecilia and Sol, destitute and homeless found shelter in an abandoned construction shack on the deserted Honixfeld property which is now 21 School Avenue. No gas, no electricity, no inside plumbing. Those in the Colony, who were in a position to help, provided coal, food and clothing for Celia and Sol. They watched Sol grow up to be a bright, industrious, young man. Sol besides being an excellent student was the chess and ping pong champion at Morris Junior College in Morristown N.J. He became a Colony legend for his ability to remain underwater for long periods of time. Sol worked his way through Morris Junior College by working nights as a janitor. On week-ends, he was the Fuller Brush salesman. This job helped put food on the table for Cecilia and Sol. Sol made accounting his life's work. He achieved the status of a Certified Public Accountant. Sol, married and enjoyed a long productive life with his wife and two daughters in Livingston, New Jersey. The Colonists were rewarded for their compassion and charity in knowing they played a part in creating a truly American success story.

CLOUDED JUDGEMENT

AT TIMES THEIR CHARITY AND compassion clouded sound judgement, common sense and decision making. Three cases of poor judgment occurred in the late 1930's and early 1940's. The executive committee in 1938 placed a help wanted ad in the Newark Evening News, {New Jersey's largest newspaper}, which read as follows, seeking "a mature man with experience in pool maintenance and supervision of young girls and boys." They selected a middle aged, unemployed gentleman from Newark, N.J. by the name of Joseph Mortimer. It wasn't long before the ten, eleven and twelve year old boys would experience an unsolicited ten week jaw-dropping, eye popping course in sex and extended lectures in the anatomical difference between girls and boys, compliments of the recently hired Joe Mortimer. Fortunately, there was never any indication of any interaction between Joe and the young people that were entrusted to him.

In September of 1938 in the lower right front page a picture and an article in the Newark Evening News shocked the Colonists. The banner over the article read, "INDICTED PEDOPHILE, JOESPH MORTIMER." The same Joseph Mortimer they hired to supervise their children. What was an embarrassment at that moment eventually became a humorous example of a very poor executive decision.

The second incident occurred in the spring of 1943. The newly created job for the sole life guard position at the Colony Pool was made known to Colony members and their children. Two people applied for the job.

Bert Abbazia, the teen age son of Oreste and Frieda and Michael Best a middle aged out of work, Colony member. The deliberations of whom to hire stretched out for a month in member's homes, casual meetings on the street and finally at the general meeting of the Colonists. The majority of the membership voted to hire Michael Best as the life guard.

1944 - Bert Abbazia, the Colony's first certified lifeguard, with his mother Frieda and sister, Diana..

The rational for selecting Best was in keeping with the member's sense of charity and compassion. The fact that Best was a family man and out of work influenced their thinking and the way they voted.

It didn't take long for everyone to realize that the membership's decision to hire Best would some day fall into the category of another bad decision and future Colony humor.

From his first day to his last day as a life guard, Best's life guard attire was navy blue dress pants, an ironed white dress shirt, black dress leather shoes, white socks and a pair of suspenders to hold up his pants. He stationed himself in a lawn chair at the shallow part of the pool. The ultimate irony was the fact that Michael Best was not a certified life guard for one simple reason. BEST DID NOT KNOW HOW TO SWIM!

P.S: Fortunately, Best never had a drowning or a near drowning while he was the life guard.

P.P.S: Bert Abbazia had certification as a life guard and as a water safety instructor. Bert was hired the next summer as the first certified life guard and water safety instructor at the pool. Bert maintained the record of never having a drowning in the years he was the life guard.

One more example of their compassion was the choice of a carpenter when the bathhouse at the pool needed repairs. The Colonists commissioned Penoff, {Last name only}, an elderly out of work Colony member with severe health problems. Penoff could barely lift a hammer let alone building materials or could he climb a ladder. His tool box consisted of one saw and one hammer, period. All Penoff's measurements were made with a rope that doubled as his belt. Before each measurement he had to untie the rope {belt} and when the measurement was satisfactorily completed, Penoff would carefully retie the rope {belt} so as to keep his pants from dropping to his knees. He kept up this untie, retie, untie, tie routine during the entire three day repair job. The untie retie routine consumed a large part of his time on the job. Penoff never wrote down a measurement, and always gave the measurement as "approximately." Penoff earned the nick name of "approximately" among the Colonists. It was spoken with affection behind his back.

These are just three examples of the Colonists of placing charity and compassion before common sense. This formula for making decisions prevailed through out the history of the Colony.

ANTI - SEMITSM

SOME JEWISH MEMBERS AND THEIR children did experience Anti- Semitism and discrimination in one form or another. Most of the Anti- Semitism was directed at the young girls in the Colony. It took the form of name calling and phrases such as "dirty Jew, Jew nose and Kike". The name calling took place mostly at school. There was a minimum of social interaction by many of the Colonists and the Township residents, young and old. No one can recall a Colony girl dating a Township boy or a Colony boy dating a Township girl.

One of the most blatant and the saddest act of discrimination was against Sol Horiwitz. Sol related his unforgettable experience sixty years later. The incident took place as part of Sol's eighth grade class trip. It was a hot June afternoon in 1933, when the bus load of cheering students pulled onto the long dirt driveway leading up to Noe's mud bottom pond. This was to be the high light of an entire day of planned activity. All the excited students were helped off the bus by the friendly driver, except one, Sol Horiwitz. As Sol was about to step off, the driver told Sol to return to his seat and remain there. He never got to swim with his classmates that day. Sol remembers breaking down and sobbing as he watched his friends enjoy his favorite sport, swimming. The driver later explained to Sol that, Jews were not welcome at Noe Pond. He was the only Jewish boy on the bus. Sol never forgot that day for as long as he lived.

RACISM

It was ironic that the pool became the background for an act of racism in the Colony. The existence of the pool in the early 1930s drew the attention of organizations from Newark seeking to conduct a day's outing in a country atmosphere. One such organization was a Negro Church from Newark. Some of the more radical members of the Colony objected strongly to allowing this group to use the pool. Some Colony Members argued that the presence of blacks would be detrimental to the value of their property. The, group, from Newark made a one time visit to the pool and were never seen again in the Colony. It seemed ironic that the Colonists who were subjected to the same discrimination would exercise Racism.

1930 – Bernard Somer and daughter Sou.

Somer's Summer School Children - Young ladies preparing to enjoy the sand baox.

FORECLOSURE

A SAD AND A PERSONAL financial set back would strike the one man in the Colony that no one thought was in a financial bind. The construction of his three story, ten room house, two car garage and the two story chicken coop proved to be too large a financial load for this Colony member. For a brief period Somer conducted a Summer School for the young children of the Colonists. The School playground consisted of one sandbox. It was in early 1932 that Hill City Building and Loan foreclosed on the largest house in the Colony. To his family and relatives, Somer's home would be forever referred to as "the big mistake." This forced the "Organizer" of the Colony to become the first victim of the Great Depression to lose his home in the Colony. No one was privy to the details of this unexpected turn of events. Did Somer over build? Was it the result of his divorce and a recent marriage? Or was it the result of all three? This sudden turn of events ended the participation and association of the "Prime Mover" and the "Organizer," Bernard Somer, to personally live out his dream as a Colonist. The "Dreamer" was now living a nightmare. He would no longer enjoy the fruits of his labor. Somer made a new life for himself with his second wife Gerty and her two daughters, Irma and Beatrice, in Plainfield New Jersey. Sou, Bernard's blind daughter from his marriage to Marie loved and depended on Bernard, but he became a part time father to Sou from the day he remarried. Sou spent the rest of her life as persona non grata to his new family. She lived with her grandmother, Jeanette, who passed away in 1941. From 1941 until Sou's death in 1991 she enjoyed the care, companionship and love of Bernard's sister, Frieda and her Cousin

Bert and his wife Theresa. Bernard Somer passed away in a Marlboro N.J. Nursing Home on May 24th, 1965 at the age of 78.

Sou passed away in 1994 at the age of 85 at the Talley Ho Nursing Home in Boonton, N.J. She will always be remembered for her ability to mesmerize her audiences of small children when reciting fairy tales. Sou developed into a gifted pianist. She readily shared her musical talent with her family, friends and the residents at The Tally Ho Nursing Home. Sou's only education came by way of reading Braille. She developed a life long love of astrology and writing poetry. Sou's gift of writing poetry culminated when her poem about man's first flight in space was acknowledged by Allen Sheppard, the astronaut.

CHANGING OF THE GUARD

THE YEAR 1933 SAW MICHAEL and Mary Rueter and their son Ralph and their daughters Ann and Mary settle in the Colony. The Rueters purchased the Pomerantz house on 10 Maple Street. Rueter quickly became a Colony member and just as quickly became very visible and very vocal at Colony meetings. Rueter demonstrated a gift for public speaking as well as the ability to rally members to his way of thinking. He was very persuasive. He quickly became the heir apparent to fill the void created when Somer left the Colony. Not only did he fill the void for many years as the day to day leader of the Colony affairs, he went on to purchase the Somer home on Lafayette Avenue. The Rueter family moved out of the Colony in the 1950's. Mary Rueter married Michael Padavano and lived in a newly built home on School Avenue.

INTRIGUE

The Colony had its share of neighborhood intrigue and mystery.

To this day, the questions, "What was Sam Greenberg's real job?" Was Sam an egg salesman or a bootlegger or both, has never been determined.

What was the relationship of Shulman and Greenberg?
Remember the infamous Jacob Shulman and family were boarders in Sam Greenberg's home leading up to the Langer murder.

What was first name only "Leaping Larry's" last name? And first name only "Old Dave's" last name?

What was last name only "Penoff's {amateur violin player} first name?

What ever happened to Stan Sherman, the guitar strumming summer visitor?

Did Shelly Rosen's friend and frequent pool visitor, Erwin Drake, ever collaborate on another hit song after "Mairzy Doats and Dozy Doats"?

What happened to Walterine, "Wally" Miller, Irv Sheib's beautiful dark haired Colony girlfriend?

Who made the communal canoe enjoyed by all the kids in the 1930's? Not much to look at, but it never leaked.

**1933 – The Communal Canoe – Jackie Gibson launching
Bobby Brindle, Bert & Milt Abbazia.**

The biggest Colony Mystery over the years, who was the inspiration and model for Ber Coffit's full body, nude statue in the middle of his pond on the corner of 326 Lafayette Avenue and Spring Street. The name of the voluptuous, nude female model remained a secret during the entire existence of the Colony. The statue was headless!

After seven decades the identity of the model can be revealed. Ber Coffit being a very talented sculptor had designed his home to include a sculpting studio. One of Coffit's greatest talents was sculpting the human head and the human body. Many of his subjects were members of the Colony and their children. Coffit's first choice for his nude model was Shirley Mollod. Shirley was the very pretty and the very shy twelve year old daughter of Harry and Ida Mollod. Coffit, for reasons unknown, never received permission from the Mollods to have Shirley pose nude for the statue. Coffit's second choice was, Evelyn Greenberg, the voluptuous, fifteen year old red haired daughter of Sam Greenberg. Colonists assumed that Coffit never received the Greenberg's consent to have Evelyn pose for "The lady in the Pond." To keep the identity of his model a secret, Coffit removed the head of the statue to conceal the identity of the model. Coffit took the secret of the headless "Lady in the Pond" to his grave.

BER COFFIT AND "THE LADY IN THE POND"

Ber Coffit and the Lady in the Pond.
Coffit's Eternal Secret

CALL TO WAR

DECEMBER 7TH, 1941, THE JAPANESE attack on Pearl Harbor, "a day in infamy" had an immediate effect on the entire country and the Colonists. A genuine wave of patriotism swept the U.S.A. Caught in the wave were Colony boys and the neighboring Township young men. It wasn't long before many of the young men answered the "Uncle Sam Wants You" recruiting campaign. Colonists and Township boys quickly answered Uncle Sam's call to duty. The majority of the eighteen to thirty five year old boys and men volunteered. Many volunteered at age seventeen and left high school without graduating. Those who did not volunteer were drafted and ended up in the Army. Whether the boys enlisted or they were drafted, it was a popular war.

Charlie Stuckelman. Irv Weiss, Bill Pomerantz, Nat Pomerantz, Gene Eisenscher, Eddie Eisenscher, Bill Kondrat, Leo Chibka, Simon Scheib, Bill and Bobby Brindle were part of those who answered Uncle Sam's call to arms. Toward the end of the war, Jerry Beauclerk, Eddie Weisgerber and Bert Abbazia joined and would become part of the "Greatest Generation." Charlie Stuckelman and Eddie Weisgerber never came back to the Colony. Charlie was killed in an unfortunate shooting incident on October 21st, 1942, while in training at the Norfolk Navel Base, and Eddie Weisgerber was killed in the invasion of Normandy on "D" day, June 6, 1944. The news of both of their deaths had an extremely sobering effect on both the old and the young in the Colony. World War II no longer was just something the Colonists saw on the newsreel at the Strand or Lyric movie theatres, the war had become personal.

EFFECTS OF WORLD WAR II

WORLD WAR II AND THE years immediately after the war saw the first signs that the future of the Colony was in jeopardy. While there was an influx of new members, their numbers were few and did not make up for the original members who had moved or passed away. The political discussions took up less and less time at the general meetings. Most of the children of the original members were growing up and leaving the Colony, never to return to participate in the operation of the Colony. The business of the Colony was being conducted, basically by the same, now older, tired members. The number of original members was dwindling. Valaria Kondrat Anjoorian, Beatrice Katz Philwin, Blanche Thorner Blumenfeld and Florence Robbins Stea were the only children of original members still residing in the Colony and taking an active role in Colony affairs. The flame that ignited the original pioneers was burning lower, political differences seemed to disappear and the only thing holding the organization together was the operation of the pool and dispersing of any surpluses to charities. The pool was a success, both socially and financially. The pool provided menial jobs for some, such as membership secretary, pool treasurer, gate keepers and a grounds management committee all come to mind. The word dissolution was now finding its way into the conversation of some members.

The 1950's and 1960's would see a building boom in Chatham Township. Noe Farm, turned into Rolling Hills. Glenmere Estates covered a vast section of the land between Fairmount Avenue and Southern Boulevard.

Wickham Woods became a popular new address. Developers cut a new street named Sunset Drive and built big, beautiful, expensive homes. New streets were cut and developed off of Fairmount Avenue. The most expensive homes in the Township were being constructed on Huron Drive and Van Houton and the connecting streets, Mohawk Terrace, Seminole Way, Ostrander Place, Rockledge Trail, and Ramapo Trail, sprung up. Noe Farm became Rolling Hills. Dale Drive, May Drive, Scenery Hill, Rolling Hill Drive, Country Club Drive and Holley Drive became a great address for the new home buyers. It was a great time to be a home owner in the Township, especially in the Colony. Why the Colony?

The Township building code required one half acre of land, 100' by 200' as a minimum building lot. All Colony lots were a minimum of one acre, 100' by 400' or 200' by 200'. A court ruling found that the Township code superseded the Colony code. Suddenly some of the members became owners of an extra, very valuable piece of real estate. Any member with a square acre, 200' by 200' could now subdivide and create two 100' by 200' building lots. It did create a windfall for those owners. A building lot, one half acre, was now selling for $15,000 to $20,000 in the Township. For ultimate privacy, Louis Robbins, the owner of three acres at the corner of Lafayette Avenue and Floral Street positioned his new house so that it impinged on all three acres. Robbins never took advantage of the Township half acre building code and the personal windfall he could have realized.

THE NEW COLONY!

A NEW COLONY WAS EMERGING in the 1950's and 1960's. The old Colony was slowly, but surely blending in with the Township and Chatham Borough. Young, affluent families were buying the new four and five bedroom, three and half bathrooms, two and three car garage homes. It was no longer a Jewish, Socialist or Communist Colony. The new home owners were, predominately Christian. The old guard had held on as long as they could. The time had come to face up to the once unthinkable, the dissolution of the Colony.

The one regret for the remaining members was relinquishing the operation of the pool and its benefits to the Colonists. The pool over the years had created an added dimension in the lives of the Colonists. They realized the pool not only provided employment for some of the members, plus many hot summer days of poolside enjoyment for all the members. The pool was realizing a profit from the guest fees. The money collected at the gate created a surplus each year. The yearly surpluses enabled the Colonists to exercise their compulsion to donate money to those in need and many worthy causes. They were a philanthropic group of people. Deciding which charities was most in need, and the most deserving, took up many hours at the Colony meetings. The larger the surplus, the longer the meetings and the more heated were the discussions. Members were divided by which charities were most deserving and what amount of money should be given each charity. Spearheaded by Fannie and Benjemin Sheib the majority favored the United Jewish Appeal {UJA}. Another group led by

Ike Eisenscher lobbied for the Long Hill fire department. Over the years, both the UJA and the Long Hill Fire Department did realize a substantial amount of the pool surplus. While the UJA and the Long Hill Department Fire were the largest beneficiaries from Colony donations, many other organizations benefitted from the pool operation.

During the period from the 1940's to 1968, The Chatham Colony Association donated over $140,000 to at least forty eight charities and individuals. In addition to their monetary donations, the Colony made available the use of the Community House for community sponsored programs. Last, but not least, the Colony donated the land that is the site of the Long Hill Fire Department's Station on Southern Boulevard. The rationale in the 1950's for the second fire station was the fact that the firemen experienced time consuming delays in responding to fires that required the River Road stationed trucks to get over "Fountain's Hill", at Fairmount Avenue or "Snake Hill" at Southern Boulevard.

THE "SEEDS" OF DISSOLUTION

THE 1960's SAW A CONTINUING loss of members, attendance at the meetings was shrinking and other than pool business, the agenda for the meetings was shrinking. The original members were approaching 60 years of age and beyond. Dissolution, the once dreaded, unthinkable word was now being discussed privately in homes and openly at Colony meetings. Many must have sought the input of their children living out of the area. The reaction of many of the children to the unthinkable word dissolution was the time had come to think of the unthinkable as very thinkable! IT WAS TIME TO LET GO! Some felt they had accomplished many of the goals their organizer, Bernard Somer had striven to achieve.

The original members, now in their mid sixties began concentrating on the dissolution of the Colony. Liquidating the assets was step number one. The assets were the pool, the Community House, the Pump House and a few acres of undeveloped land. The total number acres of Colony owned land had shrunk to seven acres. The number one condition for the sale was, "must be a suitable buyer." Their definition of a suitable buyer was someone with a strong attachment to the area and with a strong desire to continue the operation of the pool for the benefit of the residents of the Township. Getting top dollar for the assets was <u>not</u> their primary motivation.

A BARGAIN

IN A RELATIVELY SHORT TIME the Colonists came to the realization that the obvious and most suitable buyer for the pool and all their holdings was the Township of Chatham. The months that followed saw a committee of Colony members and a Township Committee, negotiate the terms of the sale. The agreed upon price was $100,000. The Township sought the approval of a bond issue of $135,000. The bond issue included one hundred thousand dollars for the purchase of the property, and thirty five thousand for pool improvements.

For the last time the Colonists had demonstrated their generosity to Chatham Township with the bargain basement price of $100,000. To support the bargain basement characterization of the sale, it must be noted that the Township was experiencing a building boom and One Hundred Thousand dollars, for seven acres of land, was unbelievably low.

November 7th, 1968, by a vote of 4 ayes to 1 nay, the bond issue passed, with the guidance of Mayor Plante! Thus ended forty seven years {16,877 days} of an endeavor to create and maintain a community within a community of nature lovers, free thinkers and a place to freely exchange political views and exercise spiritual freedom and compassion toward friends and neighbors.

THE SPOILS

EVERY COLONY MEMBER RECEIVED $5,000 for each acre of land they owned. This was the last windfall. The windfall was divided between the remaining fourteen families. Robbins the owners of three acres received $15,000. Coffit, Katz, Thorner and Abbazia each owned two acres and received $10,000. The nine members who owned one acre each received $5,000. The formality of dissolution was completed on January 1st, 1969.

The surviving fourteen members were the recipients of the final windfall. Their original investment of $162.00 an acre turned into a $5,000 an acre bonanza.

CHARITIES

The following is the list of organizations that benefited from the generosity of the Chatham Colony Association during its forty seven years of existence.

THE LIST

1. United Jewish Appeal
2. N.J-New Brunswick Retarded Children
3. N.J-Union County Retarded Children
4. N.J-Association For Retarded Children
5. Association For The Help Of Retarded Children
6. Albert Einstein Medical Center
7. Long Hill Fire Department
8. Chatham Emergency Squad
9. Madison Volunteer Ambulance Corp.
10. Community Chest
11. Morris County Heart Association
12. Middlesex County Association For The Blind
13. Morris County Mental Health
14. Eleanor Roosevelt Cancer Research
15. The Chatham Library
16. American Cancer Society
17. Chatham Township Police Athletic League
18. American Red Cross

19. U.S Commission For UNICEF
20. Channel #13
21. Jewish Child Care
22. Jewish Board Guardians
23. The Rugby School
24. Parents Council Of Retarded Children
25. The Stevens School
26. Blythedale School
27. Westchester School
28. John. F. Kennedy Memorial
29. Paraplegic Foundation Inc.
30. North American Wildlife
31. National Conference Of Christians And Jews
32. Citizens Commission For Cancer Survivors On Krebiazen
33. Hadassah Medical Relief Association
34. Overlook Hospital
35. Hadassah Trees
36. Chatham Township Anti-Jet Committee
37. March Of Dimes
38. American Cancer Society
39. Morris Junior Museum
40. Summit Chapter Of Hadassah
41. Morris County Tuberculosis Association
42. Sister Kinney
43. Weizman Institute
44. Disabled American Veterans
45. Morristown Children's Museum
46. Chatham Township's Anniversary Celebration
47. Committee To Rescue Italian Art
48. Camp Marcell
49. I.W.O International Workers Order

The donations amounted to over $140,000 over the 47 year period.

THE LEGACY

OVER THE YEARS THE COLONISTS endured sub-standard living conditions. They endured the anti-Semitic name calling. Whatever the obstacles, they rose above them. They enjoyed a frugal, modest and unassuming life style. Some rented out their homes in the summer and moved into their garage or their unused chicken coop to help make ends meet. Those who worked in New York City and had monthly train tickets on the Lackawanna railroad, made the tickets available to neighbors for a Saturday or Sunday trip into the city. They stressed the importance of an education. They encouraged and sacrificed so their children could get a college degree. They were tolerant and instilled tolerance in their children toward those less fortunate and compassion to those more oppressed. They were compassionate and generous, almost to a fault. They looked after their friends and neighbors who were experiencing hard times. They were generous with their time and money in contributing to worthy causes, both national and local. Most considered themselves as working class intellectuals. They embraced many Christian values even though most were Jewish. The majority of the Colonists were Socialists or Communists, Compassionate Socialists and Communists. They felt they were on the right side of history. After all, they were for the working man. They supported the Union movement. They opposed Hitler, Mussolini and Tojo. They had supported the Spanish Loyalists in their attempt to quell the uprising of the Fascist Dictator General Franco. They sent their children to fight in World War 11. One never did come back. They never imposed their political or religious views as an organization on their neighbors. Politics and religion were very personal and private to Colonists. They never felt their mission was to change the thinking of the residents of the Township.

Agree or disagree, they helped create Chatham Township as it exists today by consistently donating money to many of the local charities. Some volunteered locally. Ike Eisenscher was a life long booster and member of the Long Hill Fire Department. Eisenscher was also a multi gallon blood donor through the local Red Cross. Some shared their talents with the community. Caesar Stea conducted classes in art. Bertha Robbins held classes for those interested in learning Russian. The Colony made the Community House available for all their classes. The Colonists donated the land that is the site of the Long Hill Fire House on Southern Boulevard. A plaque acknowledging Ber Coffit's gift of one acre of land on Spring Street to remain as open space was dedicated on October 10th of 2010.

Last, but not least, the Colonists greatest legacy may be found in the many accomplishments of their children. The late 1940's through the early 1950's saw the off spring of the original Colonists leaving to go on to college or to start a career in business. In spite of the turmoil and uncertainty that existed in the years after World War 11, the children of the Colony went out and made their mark in the world.

SUCCESS, FAILURE, OR BOTH

How did Somer's experiment The Fourteenth Colony, end? Much like the original Thirteen Colonies, the Fourteenth Colony was integrated into the larger world surrounding it. Much like family operated enterprises, the Colony failed to survive the best efforts of the second generation. Are we to assume that Somer's experiment failed? To those Colony members who have passed on and many of those alive today, the Fourteenth Colony was a unique success. A Chatham Colony Association as a part of the world as we know the world today will never be duplicated in our time.

If the success of the Colony is to be measured by the success of the children of the original members, the experiment was a success. Most of the offspring left the Colony prepared to meet life's challenges and succeeded in their individual field of endeavor.

The list includes an osteopath, a psychologist, a lawyer, a post master. a meteorologist, an aerospace technician, an electrical engineer, a certified public accountant, an R.K.O studio illustrator, the CEO of Avnet, a Hollywood television mogul, two professors at major universities , one a professor emeritus at Cornel University, one a mathematics professor at the University of Colorado, Boulder, the manager of the family insurance business, a hospital administrator, four teachers, a financial consultant, a librarian and two entrepreneurs in the motion picture title business.

The following are the names of some, but in no way, all of the children who went on to achieve success at the highest levels in their chosen field and those with an unknown post Colony history.

WHO ARE THEY? WHERE ARE THEY?

IRVING [IZZEY, IRV] SHEIB, Irv took over the operation of his father's very successful business, Q.Q Titles. Irv and his wife Lottie had a son and a daughter. Irv and Lottie are deceased.

Mordecai [Moey] Sheib, helped his father develop Q.Q Titles, passed away at an early age from cancer. Moe was survived by his wife Dorothy and one daughter. Moe was an avid photographer. He was obsessed with taking pictures of cloud formations.

Simon Sheib, graduated Harvard University with honors, with a degree in law. Sy rose to become the CEO of Avnet, a major international corporation. Sy and Stella had one son, Sy and Stella are both deceased.

Riva Sheib Kramer, graduated from Cornell University and married Jay Kramer, a prominent labor relations attorney. Jay Kramer was appointed by three different New York Governors to sit on the three Member New York State Labor commission. Because of Kramer's reputation as being above reproach he was appointed as President of the legally entangled Del Webb Casino, Hotel in Atlantic City. After a brief period under Kramer's guidance, the Casino was relicensed and operated as the Claridge Casino, Hotel. Riva and her daughter Laura divide their time between Long Boat Key, Florida and Charlottesville, Virginia.

Their son Michael Kramer achieved great success in the literary field as an editor of "News Week" and later the editor of the New York Daily New. He has been awarded two print journalism awards by the Overseas Press Club. Kramer co-authored "I NEVER WANTED TO BE VICE PRESIDENT OF ANYTHING", the political biography of Nelson Rockefeller for which he was nominated for a Pulitzer Prize.

Michael Kramer in 2010 and 2011 focused his writing skills to authoring the Broadway Play, DEVINE RIVALRY, produced by the renowned theatrical Schubert Family. He is a graduate of Amherst College and Columbia Law School.

Sadly, Michael Kramer gained unwanted notoriety when President Clinton selected Kramer's first wife, Judge Kimba Woods, as a candidate to be the Attorney General of the United States. Judge Kimba Wood was never appointed to this high position after the disclosure that her housekeeper was an illegal alien.

Leo [Lee] Chibka, became a career civil service worker, never married. Sadly, Leo passed away at the Chibka homestead, a recluse.

Charlie Chibka, became a life-long meteorologist with the U.S Weather Bureau. Charlie was assigned to weather stations across the United States. Married, Charlie and Jan had one daughter and a son. Charlie's son is a professor at Boston College. Charlie passed away having lived a very productive life

Milton [Milt] Abbazia, graduated from the University of Alabama with a degree in Electrical Engineering in 1945. His career in electrical engineering included the largest and most prestigious companies in the world. Names like Fischbach and Moore, Howard. P. Foley, Newbury Electric, California Electric [as Vice President] and his last employer, Stiney Electric. Milt, designed and supervised major projects that included the Titan 1 Missile Base in South Dakota, the Grand Coulee Dam, Vandenberg Air Force Base,

Six Flags Magic Mountain, Universal Studios, Disney Land, California and the original M.G.M Grand Casino- Hotel in Las Vegas, Nevada. Milt married a native Los Angeles girl, Lucille Coray, and raised two daughters, Lisa and Jan. Milt passed away on March 13th, 2010 at age eighty six with an added distinction of never being retired.

Beatrice and Irma Somer: Upon leaving the Colony with Bernard and Gertie, broke off all ties with Bernard's family. No post Colony history.

Bert Abbazia, {the Author} Graduated Chatham High School. He earned 11 varsity letters in three sports, baseball, soccer and basketball. Bert was selected to the 1944 second team All State Soccer team and the first team, group one, All State 1945 basketball team. Upon his discharge from the U.S. Navy, Bert entered Seton Hall College. He became a member of the Seton Hall Soccer team as a "walk on" and led the 1948 undefeated team in scoring. His single season record of 20 goals remained unbroken for 14 years. In the year 1949, at age 21, Bert founded Done-Well Cleaners and graduated Seton Hall. Two months after his 22nd birthday Bert married his high school sweetheart, the beautiful, Theresa Romano. They have three daughters, Linda Abromitis, a real estate broker, Loralee Beard, founder of Magic Moment Photography in Grayson Georgia and Janet Abbazia Petzel, Vice President of Turner Broadcasting Special Events, 6 grandchildren and 6 great grandchildren. Bert has been a real estate agent since 1986. In keeping in the tradition of his Uncle Bernard Somer, Bert, during his tenure of seventeen years on the New Providence Recreation Commission, spearheaded the development of the country club of town pools, the New Providence Community Pool and the New Providence Tennis courts.

Diana Abbazia Holdridge, after graduating Chatham High School, Diana went on to earn a degree from the University of Pennsylvania. Upon graduation Diana became the office manager for New York Congressman Theodore Kupferman. Diana married Steve Holdridge and has a son, Jim, in Hollywood and a daughter Heather in Washington D.C. Steve and

Diana make Wilmington North Carolina their home and where Diana continues her career as a realtor.

Charlie Stuckelman, joined the Navy and was killed October 21st, 1942 off the base while in basic training in Norfolk Virginia. The details of his death were never shared with the Colonists. Charlie had to be one of Chatham High School's greatest Soccer goalies.

William [Billy] Pomerantz, joined the United States Air force and became a fighter pilot during World War 11. Upon his discharge Billy operated a hot dog cart in Newark New Jersey. Deceased

Nathan [Nate] Pomerantz, joined the Army during World War 11. Upon his discharge, Nat worked his way through the U.S postal system and became a Postmaster before his retirement. Deceased

Eugene [Red] Eisenscher, Gene's attendance at Rutgers University was interrupted when he enlisted in the submarine service in World War 11. Upon his discharge he joined Philco Aerospace and continued to serve his country by maintaining U.S. Army radio transmitters and electronic systems in the Far East. Upon returning to the states, Gene's career with Philco continued as the first sales engineer working with major companies on the application of semiconductors in military and space programs. He was the proud recipient of many U.S Government citations. He was a proud veteran of the Submarine Service. After his retirement, Gene and his wife Mitzi devoted their lives to assisting senior citizens in nursing homes with financial guidance. Gene and Mitzi spent many happy years discovering America. Upon Gene's death, he was accorded the high honor of being interred in Arlington National Cemetery.

Howard {Howie} Frankel, No post Colony history.

Mildred Eisenscher Cornzewit: Mildred graduated a Newark, N..J. State teacher's college and became a career librarian. Mildred and her husband Ernie, have passed away leaving one son, Danny and a daughter.

Augusta Coffet Dunn: Became a nurse.

Denora Coffit: Enjoyed life as an artist in N.Y.C.

Sigmond, Edward, No post Colony information. Deceased.

Ester Eisenscher: No post Colony information.

Irving Weiss, Irv served in World War Two in the United States Army and was discharged as a Lieutenant. He earned a degree in mathematics at the University of Michigan after transferring from Columbia University. Irv went on to become a mathematics professor at the University of Colorado Boulder. Irv passed away on May 5th, 2011 in Boulder. Irv and wife Marjorie had three daughters, Ellen, a teacher, Wendy, a coffee shop manager and Deborah, Executive Director of Alumni Affairs. Because of his amazing memory of Colony history and his life achievements, Irv deserves the distinction of being recognized as MISTER COLONY.

Isadore Blumen: The Blumen family moved out of the Colony when he was age nine. Upon graduating High School, Isadore served in the Army in World War 11. After his discharge from the Army Isadore entered and graduated from the University of North Carolina with a PHD in Mathematical Statistics. He retired as a professor emeritus from Cornell University. He and his wife Mary have two daughters. Isadore has two childhood memories of the Colony. The first, drinking water delivered by truck and the second, the first speed bump on Main Street, Chatham Borough.

Doiv and Benjimin Barlus: No post Colony information.

The Langer Family: Morris Langer's wife and daughters, Ruth and Florance moved out of the Colony shortly after his death. They took up residence in New York City.

Gerald Beauclerk, "Cherries": Married "Rusty" Beneduce of Madison, N.J and moved to Charlotte, North Carolina. They had one son. Sadly, their son passed away at an early age. Jerry has passed away.

Dorothy Beauclerk: Married Ted Williams, not the baseball player. Dorothy had a son, Gilbert Nyer, from a World War 11 romance. Dorothy is deceased.

Jackie Gibson: Jackie was rumored to have tried following in his fathers footsteps as an actor on the New York stage.

Soloman [Sol] Gibson: No post Colony information on Solly.

Sanford Shulman: Eventually moved to California.

Alex Koukley: Upon graduating high school Alex joined the U.S Army and served during World War 11. Alex made a career as a financial consultant. He is retired and lives in Florida.

Eugenia Koukley: Graduated New York University with a degree in Physical Education and taught in the New York School system. Eugenia finished her professional career at a nursery school. She and her husband, Dick, have two children and live in Boynton Beach Florida.

Judy Greenberg: What did happen to the queen of the Colony Pool? Judy was married three times, first to Herb Silver, a very handsome, successful, accountant. Judy's second marriage was to Ted Ellis a Sears, Roebuck vice president. Her third marriage was to the Attorney General for the state of Idaho. Judy passed away in her mid eighties. She has one married daughter, Karen Heppin and one son, Joseph, an attorney.

Lou Cohn: Lou graduated from Cooper Union College and continued his education in med- school. Lou spent many successful years as a respected osteopath. Dr. Lou and his wife, Ann, had four sons, Bill, Charlie, Allen and Danny. They are all well-established dentists and doctors. Bill is a very successful dentist in Westchester, N.Y. Charlie does geriatric social work in Israel and has 20 grand children. Danny is a radiologist. Allen is an internist.

Ralph Rueter: Upon his discharge from the Navy, Ralph went on to attain a Gold Seal rating as an air conditioning specialist for hospitals in California. Deceased

Mary Rueter Padavanno: Went to Oak Knoll School in Summit N.J. Mary married Mike Padavanno and helped manage their very successful restaurant, The Blue Shutters, in Union N.J. for many years.
Mike and Mary have two daughters.

Ann Rueter: Trained for a nursing career at St. Michaels Hospital in Newark N.J. Ann went on to become a cadet nurse during World War 11. Ann Rueter, passed away early in life.

Ioletta Kondrat: Received a scholarship to the New Jersey College for Woman and received her degree in education. Ioletta was salutatorian of C.H.S class of 1945. Ioletta had one daughter. Ioletta has since passed away.

Valaria Kondrat Anjoorian: Married with one son, Jason. Spring Street, Chatham Township is still her address.

William [Valutchic] Kondrat: Upon his discharge from the Army in World War Two as a Lieutenant, Valutch married Frieda Blumenthal and had one son, William Junior. Valutch went into the business of raising chickens in Paso Robles, California. He eventually worked at the Department of Mental Hygiene in Atascadero, California. Valutch passed away in 1987 in an assisted living facility in California at the age of seventy two.

Iola Schipler: Upon graduation, Iola continued in her pursuit of a career in music. She played the violin in many venues in N.J. She made an appearance at The Mosque theatre in Newark, N.J.

Beatrice Katz Philwin: Upon graduating C.H.S, Bea attained a Bachelors of Arts and Masters degree from CCNY. Bea went on to attain her PHD at Arizona State University in Psychology. She still resides in the original Katz's home on Lafayette Avenue. Bea and her husband, Howie, have a son Jed, a lawyer, and two daughters, Leslie and Stephanie.

Gabriel [Gabe] Katz: Left Chatham and graduated Washington Irving H.S in New York City. At age 17 Gabe was employed by RKO studios as an illustrator. Gabe became well known in the illustrator world as Gabe Karden. Gabe's career as an illustrator led to a brief encounter with Timothy Leary, the advocate of psychedelic ecstasy drugs, during the Hippie Era. This brief, casual acquaintance ended with Katz moving to New Mexico. Gabe never married.

Blanche Thorner Blumenfeld: Upon graduating Chatham High School, Blanche went on to receive a bachelors and a master's degree in education from New York University. Blanche married Fred and had two children. Her daughter Karen is a lawyer and her son, Daniel is a Doctor.

Estelle Stuckelman Greenburg: Upon graduation, Estelle found employment at Beth Israel Hospital in Newark N.J. Estelle worked her way up in the medical field, attained and held the position of administrator at Beth Israel for 15 years. Estelle was married to Jerry Greenburg. They are the parents of 4 successful daughters. Estelle lives in South Orange N.J.

Sylvia Stuckelman: Became a nurse at Beth Israel hospital in Newark N.J. Sylvia has passed away.

Milton White: No post Colony history.

Boozie Bernstein: No post Colony history.

Bernard [Bernie] Mollod: Graduated Staunton Military Academy. Bernie enlisted in the U.S. Air force in World War 11. Upon his discharge, he entered into the very successful family insurance business. Bernie is retired in Long Island, N.Y. He and his son own and operate an ocean front motel in Miami Beach and a shopping center in Tennessee.

Shirley Mollod: Married a successful doctor and lives in Chevy Chase Maryland.

Gloria Schwartz: No Post Colony Information.

Sheldon Rosen: Upon leaving the Colony, Sheldon Rosen became Sheldon Reynolds. Besides being the best jitterbug and shag dancer in the Colony, Shelly became a renowned Hollywood writer, director, actor and producer. He produced a Sherlock Holmes – Doctor Watson series. Shelly is best known for his 1950's hit T.V series Foreign Intrigue. It was the fore-runner for many T.V adventure series to follow. On a personal note, Shelly's wife, Andrea Plunkett Reynolds, ended their marriage when she became the mistress of Klaus von Bulow. The same Klaus von Bulow of Sunny Von Bulow infamy. Shelly Rosen Reynolds passed away in 2005.

Evelyn Greenburg: No post Colony information.

Sol Horiwitz: Upon graduation from Chatham High School, Sol continued his education at Morris Junior College in Morristown N.J. Sol earned his degree as an accountant and eventually practiced his profession as a very successful certified public accountant. He and his wife had a daughter. Sol has passed away.

The perception in the Township and the Borough was that the Colony children were among the brightest students at the Red Brick, Southern Boulevard and Chatham High Schools. They earned the respect of teachers Margaret Belcher. Gladis Bahoosian, Grace Herbert and George Osbourne, the Principal, for their class room achievements. This perception would later be substantiated by the number who went on to college and by their eventual success in the real world. The future looked bright and promising for the post World War 11 generation, or did it?

THE CLOUD

LIKE EVERY GENERATION, THE COLONIST'S off spring left with mixed emotions, uncertainty, trepidation, anticipation, hope and in some cases, unfounded confidence. Little did they realize how much the freedom, the discipline, the constant pursuit of education and the ability to live with people with diverse life styles and ideas had prepared them for the real world. At this time of their lives they were unaware of an ominous cloud that could and would possibly effect, their lives and the lives of any friends and acquaintances for years to come.

The cloud was the creation of Joseph McCarthy, the junior senator from Wisconsin. The 1950's would see Senator McCarthy orchestrate an anti-Communist mood in America. McCarthy's claims of wide spread Communist spies and subversive organizations infiltrating government agencies and even the halls of Congress attracted many believers and followers. As the chairman of the Senate Permanent Sub Committee on Investigations, McCarthy conducted many baseless investigations and slandered many innocent individuals and organizations. His conduct and his unethical abuse of his power created the term, McCarthyism. McCarthyism became synonymous with the term Witch Hunt. McCarthy's investigations reached from the inner circles of Hollywood and Broadway to the cloak room of the Senate Chambers. Anyone in Hollywood and Broadway, from directors, actors and stage hands, once branded and slandered as a Red Sympathizer were banned from pursuing their show biz careers for years. McCarthy investigation purged the television industry and the print media. Well known columnists and reporters, in the print media, found themselves to be persona non grata and unemployable for years.

His downfall began with his investigation of the U.S Army and specifically the Signal Corp at Fort Monmouth, N.J. The renowned attorney, Joseph Welsh, in the 1954 nationally televised Senate hearing exposed McCarthy as a fraud and a man "of no decency." McCarthy was eventually censured by Congress. Disgraced and ignored by Congress, Joe McCarthy at the age of 48 passed away from acute Hepatitis, an inflammation of the liver as a result of alleged alcoholism. Part of McCarthy's legacy was the creation of a list of individuals and organizations believed to be Communist sympathizers and followers. McCarthy claimed to possess a list of 57 Communists and Communist sympathizers in government. He failed to produce one person with any Communist connection to the Senate investigating committee. Many Colonists in the 1950's, 1960's and to the day they die will always believe that the Colony and its members were on the infamous list. How did this possible labeling effect the Colonists and their children and anyone connected or associated with them through friendship or marriage? Many disassociated themselves from the Colony when applying for a job or in a sensitive situation. The possibility of an investigation and retaliation by a government agency became a constant concern and threat to many who feared their name might be on the Phantom List.

TIME TO LET GO

The Colony in the 1950's was becoming the victim of member attrition. Fewer members meant fewer people to conduct Colony business. The, Business, of the Colony was primarily the operation of the pool and the dispersing of any surplus monies. Valaria Kondrat Anjoorian, Beatrice Katz Plilwin, Blanche Thorner Blumenfeld and Florance Robbins Stea continued to be the only children of original Colonists still residing in the Colony and taking an active role in Colony affairs.

Slowly, but surely, the dwindling membership was awakening to the realization that the time to let go was drawing near. Many felt they had attained the life style their Organizer,"Bernard Somer was striving to achieve.

The Colony was no longer the Colony of the 1920's, 30's, 40's, or 50's. The memories of those years still smolder in the minds of those who experienced those unforgettable years. It is understandable that the recollections of the sons and daughters are not always the same.

Most Colony boys felt the Colony environment enabled them to enjoy many carefree days, fresh air, a pool, open fields, outdoor fun and games. Friendly paths, and short cuts through friendly woods, good friends and the feeling of unrestricted freedom. It couldn't get any better.

In sharp contrast, many of the girls in the Colony were subjected to the local anti-Semitism, restrictions in their social life and the lack of opportunity to pursue their hobbies and fulfill their dreams. Their perception of Colony life created a need to look beyond the Colony for a better tomorrow. It is interesting to note, the only marriage to materialize in the Colony was the wedding of Estelle Stuckelman to Jerry Greenberg, the younger brother of Judy Greenberg. It is also interesting to note that as of the year 2010, three children of the original members never moved from the Colony, all daughters, all living at their parent's original address. They are Dr. Beatrice Katz Philwin, Lafayette Avenue, Blanche Thorner Blumenfeld, Maple Street and Valarie Kondrat Anjoorian, Spring Street.

THE TRANSFORMATION

IN LOOKING BACK, THE YEARS between 1921 through 1941, the beginning of World War 11, best epitomized the life style Somer and the original Colonists envisioned. It was during this period, they created their own community, the roads, the Community House, the water supply, the pool, the ball field, and their own way of life. The members went through the good times and the bad times together. They assimilated into the community and helped make Chatham Township a magnet for families seeking safety, access to major highways and Newark International Airport, public transportation to New York City, diversified recreation, an excellent school system and competent management of local government.

Slowly, many of the original members transformed themselves from Communists, Socialists and Trotskyites to Democrats, Republicans and Independents and, most significant, they became valuable American citizens.

THINGS REMEMBERED,
THE 1920's, 1930's AND 1940's

SLEDS:

Flexible Flyer

BICYLES:

Schwinn
Raliegh
Ivor- Johnson

Motor Cycles:

Harley Davidson
Indian

AIRLINES:
Eastern
American
United
Pan American

MOVIE STARS:

Charlie Chaplin	Mickey Rooney
Mae West	Ann Rutherford
Tom Mix	The Barrymores
Wallace Beery	Al Jolson
Margorie Main	Eddie Cantor
Boris Karloff	Bela Lugosi
Rudolf Valentino	Shirley Temple
Sonja Heine	

William Boyd, {Hop along Cassidy}

Jackie Cooper: "Our Gang" fame.

MAJOR NEWS EVENTS, 1020's, 1930's, 1940's:

Sacco and Venzetti, "Red Scare," Tried and executed 1927

Holland Tunnel opens in 1927

Lindbergh Flies Solo across the Atlantic, 1927

Stock Market Crash, 1928

Franklin Delano Roosevelt elected President, 1932

Hughie Long assassinated, 1935

Lindbergh's infant son kidnapped, 1932

Hindenburg crashes and burns off of Asbury Park, N.J and Lowell Thomas makes his famous, emotional eye witness radio report to the nation, 1937

Adolph Hitler came to power in Germany, 1930's

Benetto Mussolini came to power in Italy, 1920's

Orson Wells October 30th, 1938, created mass national hysteria with the radio broadcast of a fictitious alien invasion. The program was called "War of the Worlds."

AUTOMOBILES:

Ford
Plymouth
Chevrolet

CIGARETTES:

Camels, "I'd walk a mile for a Camel"

Chesterfields, "The Pause That Refreshes"
Arthur Godfrey, spokesman

Philipp Morris, "Johnny" calling out "Call for Philipp Morris" to the theme song, On the Trail

CANDY BARS:

Hershey's Chocolate
Baby Ruth

SODA

Coca Cola
Pepsi Cola
Ginger Ale

BREAKFAST CEREAL:

Kellogg's Corn Flakes and Rice Krispies
Kasha
Wheaties

CAMERAS:

Kodak, Box and Folding
No one took pictures at Colony events. Movie cameras weren't prevalent
in the 1920's and 1930's.

ENTERTAINMENT IN THE 1920's, 1930's, AND 1940's:

RADIO PROGRAMS:

Tom Mix   The Lone Ranger
Let's Pretend   The Shadow
Uncle Don   Just Plain Bill
Lowell Thomas   Father Coughlin
Jack Armstrong, "All American Boy"
Metropolitan Opera of The Air
John B. Gambling, WOR Radio, "Rambling with Gambling." Announced
school closings and featured the World's Greatest Little Orchestra.

BIG BAND THEATERS:

The Paramount Theater, Times Square, N.Y.C.

Adams Theatre, Newark, N.J.

Frank Daly's Meadowbrook, Pompton Turnpike, N.J.

LOCAL ENTERTAINMENT:

Madame Bey's Training Camp, River Road, C.T.

Tobey's Comedians, Long Hill Firehouse

Donkey Baseball, Sponsored by the Chatham Boro Fire Department

Hunt Brother's Circus, One Ring Circus, C.B.

Bertrand's Island, Lake Hopatcong, N.J.

Olympic Park, Featuring Bubbles, the singer, Joe Basile's Band and one circus act, Irvington N.J.

SUMMER TIME TREATS:

Chewing on a small glob of day old tar after a road had been freshly tarred. The tar was a tasty substitute for Wrigley's gum

Chipping and stealing chips of ice from Muchmore Brothers ice truck

Eating a burnt black potato, fresh from the red hot ashes of a campfire

Roasting Campfire Marshmallow on an open fire

Eating fresh vegetables from neighbor's gardens

Scooping up fresh, cool, clear water, by hand, from the lazy stream that flowed through the swamp for a hot summer time thirst quencher

Picking and eating huckleberries in the Swamp

SCENTS:

The smell of burning leaves in the fall

Burnt toast in the morning.

The aroma of freshly mown hay

Carnations at Nauman's Greenhouses

Roses at Noe's Greenhouse

SOUNDS:

Herman and Red Nauman punctually sounding the weekday 12: Noon and 5:00 pm Siren at the Nauman Greenhouses

The warning bell of an approaching Trolley on Main Street, Chatham Boro

The whaling siren emanating from the Long Hill Fire House and the raspy sounding horn from the Green Village Fire House to alert the volunteers of a fire

The banging and flapping of a broken snow chain against the inner fender of a car on a snowy day

The yell, "SHINE", by the shoe shine men, all in matching, black shirts, pants and caps on the Barcley Street Ferry

The eerie whistle of the D.L&W steam engine going through Chatham on a damp, humid morning, accurately forecasting an eminent rain storm

The horrendous bomb blast on March 23rd, 1933 announcing the assassination of Morris Langer

The gentle ringing of the bell attached to the neck of the Bell Cow leading the herd back to Noe's barns in time to be hand milked at 4:00 pm

The shrill two finger whistle of a father summing his child home

The magnificent voice emanating from the public address announcer at Grand Central Station, heralding the arrival and departure of the 20ᵗʰ Century Limited to and from far off places across the forty eight states

The Colony children enjoyed American patriotic songs, America the Beautiful and The Star Spangled Banner. They were familiar with the words and music of radical, militant songs from foreign countries. The inspiring French National Anthem, LA MARSELILLE, Russia's revolutionary song LENIN IS OUR LEADER and BANDIER ROSSA, the Italian Communist, rallying song, were part of the musical memories of many of the young and old in the Colony

The Colonists enjoyed Irving Berlin's patriotic World War 1 songs, Over there and Oh, How I Hate To Get Up In the Morning. They joined the rest of the country in singing Eddie Cantor's depression hit, Now Is the time to Fall In Love

SIGHTS:

Cars with running boards and rumble seats

The Trolley Cars traveling through Chatham to Newark and back until the 1930's. The abandoned tracks were removed and the steel was used for the manufacture of ships and tanks for the war effort during World War 11

Horse droppings on the roads of the Township

The horse trough on South Passaic Street next to Caufield's Bar, {now Charlies Aunt} C.B.

Amber street lights on Main Street, Madison. A 1930's, 1940's experiment for better vision in fog

The sight of thousands of homeless, unemployed men, Aimlessly, congregating around open fires and tin roofed card board box shelters along the route of the Polaski Skyway through Secaucus, to New York City in the 1930's {Now I-95, the Turnpike]

BRANDS OF ICE CREAM:

Bryers

Castles, Dixie Cups with pictures of Major League Baseball players on the lids

Eskimo Pies

SNAKE HILL, TEST TRACK:

Snake Hill, Chatham Township.
Prior to Oldsmobile Motors developing the Automatic Transmission {Hydro-Matic} in the 1940's, all cars had "stick shifts." The stretch of Southern Boulevard from River Road to Fairmount Avenue was appropriately called Snake Hill. A bird's eye view of the 200 yards of the road showed the road did resemble a slithering snake. The sharp curves and steep incline did present a challenge to all cars and most young drivers. The average car could not get to the top of the hill in high gear. The challenge for every beginner was learning to shift from high gear to second gear, without the car stalling. Snake Hill was the ultimate test for beginners. Snake Hill was Chatham Township's Pikes Peak. The Township in the 1950s did realign the road and effectively removed the snake from Snake Hill

POLICE FORCE:

Chief Herbert Rowe, a one man police force, investigated Langer's murder

Chief Rustum Bey, a one man police force, son of Madame Bey, of Madame Bey's Training Camp fame

TRAPPING, WITH STEEL TRAPS:

Setting traps along the banks of the Passaic River and in the Great Swamp to catch and skin muskrats. Getting up at 4: am to check the trap line. Skins were sent to Sears and Roebuck in Chicago, Illinois. They paid fifty cents to one dollar for a muskrat skin

Learning to identify animals by their tracks

APPLIANCES:

Stoves, Coal or Kerosine

Insect Extermination, fly swatter and sticky fly paper

Lawn mower, silent, push hand mowers

Clothes Dryer, a rope, hung between two trees in a backyard.

Refrigeration: Ice Box

Clothes Washer, Scrubbing Board

R.C.A Victor Victrola, first demonstrated in 1925

SWAMP BOARDWALK:

The Boardwalk was three 2" by 10" boards. Ten inches in width and two inches thick. It originated near Southern Boulevard and ended at Long Hill Lane. It was built in the 1930's by the Civilian Conservation Core, {CCC}. The boardwalk was constructed beneath the power lines to provide walking access to the power lines in the Great Swamp

LUNCHEONETTES:

Harry's Store, Fairmount Avenue, C.T.

Botti's Store, Green Village Road, C.T.

CABLE SYSTEM:

The long outdoor cable transporting milk in cans from the cow barns to the pasteurizing and processing shed at Noe Farm

WORLD WAR TWO MEMORIES.

RATIONING:

World War Two saw the Government Issue rationing books. The books contained coupons which entitled the bearer to limited amounts of sugar, meat, flour, gasoline, nylon stockings, coffee, butter and many of the essentials for living

PRACTICE BLACKOUTS:

The air raid siren that signaled the mandatory extinguishing of all lights. This was enforced by volunteer neighborhood air raid wardens. Chatham's legendary air raid warden was, Black Out MacArthur.

ANCHOR CHAIN FACTORY:

Anchor chains for the Liberty Ships were manufactured at Chatham Engineering on Willow Street, C.B, in the 1940's. Now the site of the Willows a high end condominium complex on Schindler Court

MACHINE SHOP:

The war years, 1941 to 1945, saw, Harry Cooper, the new owner of the Barlus home at 18 School Avenue turn his basement into a machine shop

Cooper and his family along with hired help in the Colony manufactured parts for the Army to aid in the war effort. The machine shop closed soon after the Japanese surrendered on August 14th, 1945

PLACES TO SOCIALIZE

DANCING:

Meyersville Grange Hall
Square dancing on Friday nights, Still there.
No more Friday night square dances.
Occasional flee market on Sunday.

THE MEYERSVILLE GRANGE HALL, 2010

Meyersville Grange Hall
Great Memories

BOWLING:

Farley's Bowling Allies, Morris Avenue, Springfield. Currently the Short Hills Caterers.

Madison Lanes, Lincoln Place, Madison

ROLLER SKATING:

Morris and Essex Roller Rink. Morris Turnpike, Springfield. Currently, site of Bed, Bath and Beyond.

Florham Park Roller Rink, Brook Lake Road Florham Park

HORSEBACK RIDING:

Three 10 year old boys riding Joe Staszak's Swayback Horse, Joe, around Noe's cow barns, together. No Saddle

FIELD DAY:

The annual Colony day of games and races at the athletic field for the younger boys and girls. The big prize was a model airplane kit or a Paddle Ball game. [A small rubber ball connected to a wooden paddle by an elastic band]

HOLIDAYS:

The Jewish Holidays, Passover, Rosh Hashanah, Yom Kippur, Purim and Hanukkah, were observed by many Colonists

May Day, May 1st and Labor Day, a Union Holiday, were celebrated by many Colonists. These two holidays seemed to receive greater recognition from Colonists than Memorial Day.

PLACES REMEMBERED!
1920's, 1930's

GROCERY STORES:

The Great Atlantic and Pacific, Main St., C.B.
The entire store was smaller than the soft drinks isle in today's modern super markets. Salvatore {Doe} Pagliara, the clerk, retrieved all the customer's selections from shelves behind the counter

King's Market	Springfield Ave, Summit
Grand Union	Main St, C.B.
National Store	Main Street, C.B.

CLOTHING STORES:

Marx's Department Store	Adjacent to the Chatham Public Library, Main St, C.B.

HARDWARE STORES:

Marenghi's Hardware	Main St, C.B.
Trowbridge and Attridge	Main St, C.B.

ICE CREAM PARLORS, LUNCHEONETTES:

Main Drugs	Corner, Main Street and No. Passaic Ave, C.B.
Chiefs	Main St, C.B.
Sweet Shop	Main St, C.B.
Bernstein's Drug Store	Springfield Ave, Summit

AUTOMOBILE REPAIR GARAGES:

Scherer's Garage.	So. Passaic Ave, Next to Railroad Bridge
Kelly's Garage	No. Passaic Ave, C.B.

MOVIE THEATRES:

Summit Strand	Springfield Ave, Summit, Now a Mini Mall
Madison Strand	Lincoln Pl., Madison
Lyric Theatre	Beechwood Rd, Summit Destroyed by fire, 1940's.

Train ride AND admission to anyone of the three theatres, was twenty five cents in the 1930's

DINERS:

Goumas's Diner	Main St. Madison
Chatham Diner	Main St, C.B.

AMUSEMENT PARKS:

Olympic Park	Irvington, N.J. Joe Basile Band and Bubbles the singer were featured
Coney Island	New York, famous for the parachute jump

BARBER SHOPS:

Mercer's Barber Shop	South Passaic Ave., C.B.
Nick and Art	Main St., C.B.

LIBRARY:

Chatham Library	Main Street, C.B.

SHOEMAKERS:

Gazzetto	South Passaic Ave., C.B.
Pagliara's	North Passaic Ave., C.B.

LUMBER YARD:

Fred. L. Walter's And Son, Coal and Lumber Co.
River Rd., C.B

GAS STATIONS:

Karl Koehler Sunoco	Fairmount Ave, C.T.
De Santis Texeco	Main St., C.B.
Quackenbush Shell	Main St., C.B.

NEWSPAPER STORE:

Paterson's Cigar and Liquor Store   Corner, Main St. and
So. Passaic Ave., C.B

Henrich Newspaper stand   Chatham railroad station

BANK:

Chatham Trust   Main St., C.B.

TAVERNS:

Hirsch's Tavern   Main St. Near River, C.B.

Rillo's Tavern   River Rd., C.B.

DRY CLEANERS AND LAUNDRIES:

Utility Laundry   Main St., C.B, {Near Passiac River}

Chatham Cleaners   Main St., C.B. {Sam Siegel owner}

RESTAURANTS:

William Pitt   Main St., C.B.

BASEBALL TEAMS:

New York Yankees
Brooklyn Dodgers   {All New York Teams}
New York Giants

Newark Bears Newark, N.J.

BICYCLE SHOP:

    Mutter   North Passaic Ave., C.B.

SCHOOL BUS COMPANIES:

    Hinds   Green Village Rd.
                           Green Village C.T.

    Weber   River Rd., Long Hill, C.T.

FUNERAL HOME:

    Martinus Funeral Home   Main St., C.B.

REAL ESTATE AGENCY:

    Kimball Coleman Agency   Main St., C.B.

BIG BANDS:

    Benny Goodman
    Tommy Dorsey
    Glenn Miller
    Artie Shaw

BAKERY:

    Scherer's Bakery   South Passaic Ave., Next
                          to Scherer's Garage, C.B.

    Chatham Bake Shop   Main St., C.B.

FLORIST:

Sunnywood Florist   Jared Moore owner,
                              So. Passaic Ave., C.B.

FIVE AND TEN CENT STORE:

Dodge's   Main St., C.B.

TURKEY FARM AND MINK RANCH:

Josa's Turkey Farm   Pine St., C.T..

Mr. Vital's Mink Ranch   Now 12 Pine St., C.T.
                              In operation until demolished
                              by a ??? fire in the late 1930's.

HORSE TROUGH AND DRINKING FOUNTAIN:

So. Passaic Ave., Next to Caulfield's Bar {Now Charlie's Aunt} C.B.

DRUG STORE:

Main Drugs   Corner Main St., and N. Passaic
                              Ave., C.B.

HOT DOG STANDS:

Rudy's   Watchung Ave.,
                              Next to Passaic River, C.B.

Kenny's   Hotdogs boiled in oil.
                              Morris Turnpike, Summit

BASEBALL FIELDS:

Colony Field	School Ave., Next to tower line, Currently the tennis courts. C.T.
Noe's Field	Noe Ave. Next to the original Doremus Estate, C.T. Currently site of mansions

SLEIGH RIDING HILLS:

Hutchie's Lane, named after the Hutchinson Family, living on the corner of Fairview Ave. and Lafayette Ave., C.T.

Breger's Field, Lafayette Ave., Named after the original owners, the Bregers. Now the site of Chatham H.S and the Board Of Education Office. C.T.

Monkey Lane, A.K.A. Longwood Ave., name origin unknown, C.T.

PATHS AND SHORTCUTS:

Walking through back yards, tree-lined paths and shortcuts through safe and friendly woods to a friend's home, the pool or to school

VEGETABLE STAND:

Fornaro's Stand	Southern Boulevard, Still in existence as of the year, 2011, C.T.

FORNARO'S ROADSIDE VEGATABLE STAND 2010

Fornaro's Vegetable Stand

RESALE SHOP:

Arhie,s Resale,   Meyersville Rd., Gillette
                       No longer in existence

EXOTIC ANIMAL FARMS:

Phifer's Animal Farm, Morristown Rd., Gillette home to many exotic wild animals. Remembered as the home of Hollywood's M.G.M Lion, Leo. Leo's bones are interred near the front door of Zolney Phifer's, abandoned farm house

2011 - Phifer's Deserted Animal Farm

Henry Krajewski's pig farm in Secaucus, N.J. Notable for the stench emanating from the pig farm when driving route #22 through Secaucus to New York City in the 1930's

LOVERS LANE:

The dirt road under the high tension lines off of Mount Vernon Avenue, C.T. Was part of the Sam Everett Estate. Currently the site of the Chatham Glen sprawling condominium complex

DEPARTMENT STORES:

L. Bamberger, Newark, N.J.
Orhbach, Newark, N.J.
Kresge, Newark, N.J.
S. Kline on The Square, Newark, N.J.

PUBLIC TRANSPORTATION:

Morris Trolley, 1920's and 1930's
Lackawanna Railroad
Public Service Bus, #70 to Newark, post trolley cars

SCHOOL JANITOR:

The Southern Boulevard School janitor, Mr. Ortley Emerging out of the janitor's room to accept his annual Christmas gift, a box of cigars.

MARBLES

Playing marbles, For Keeps from the day the robins arrived back for their Northern vacation until Halloween. Marble season was dirty knuckle season for marble enthusiasts

SUMMER ATTIRE:

Latex bathing suits replaced the never drying suits of the 1930's. The Latex bathing suit became 24/7 wearing apparel for many of the Colony boys during July and August

COMIC BOOKS:

"Big Little Books", measuring 3 and 5/8"by 4" and ½" and 1/1/2" thick were popular with the Colony boys in the 1930's. The books sold for 10 cents and were the forerunner of today's 6.625" x 10.25" comic books

NEW YORK TREATS:

Nedicks, a hot dog and orange drink, 15 cents. "Better than Nathans." The chain of the Popular 1930's and 1940's stores has been reduced to one location in Penn Station, N.Y.C.

Horn and Hardart Automats: Purchase each item by inserting nichols in the coin slot by the small window that attractively displayed each food treat individually

MOVING AND STORAGE COMPANY:

Chatham Movers, the Sacco family owned and operated the business for decades

SECURITY SYSTEM:

The hissing, snapping bite of geese was as effective as the bite of a vicious dog for protecting a home owners property. Beauclerk's geese made effective watch dogs. The geese were more effective in keeping strangers from coming on to their property than Pete, their old mutt

PIANO TEACHER:

Mrs. Smith, Lafayette Ave., C.B.

CHILDREN'S DANCE STUDIO:

Wealthy Ann Townsend, Lafayette Avenue, C.T.
Wealthy Ann was the wife of Charlie Wittreich, son of the respected Pine Street Wittreich family

COLONY ROMANCE:

Irv Sheib and Walterine {Walley} Miller. Irv had movie star looks and Walley was a Dark haired beauty

HITCH HIKING:

Learning the art of "hitching a ride" was a must for every teenage boy. William Kondrat accumulated the most "frequent hitchhiker" miles. He also mingled with the Hobos when riding freight cars.

CHICKEN COOPS:

Most of the chicken coops in the Colony were one story, ground level. Thorner had three chicken coops. The hen house was 2 stories high. Eisenscher built the "Empire State Building" of chicken coops, it was 3 stories high and almost a hundred feet in length

TELEPHONE SERVICE:

Slowly in the 1930's the Colonists discovered the telephone. Most of the Colonists subscribed to an economical phone service called the Party Line. The Party Line bundled up to ten subscribers on one line. Common courtesy encouraged a caller to limit their conversations to five minutes in cases where another caller was attempting a call. The more parties sharing a telephone number, the more economical the monthly rate. Most colonists subscribed to the four party plan and some took advantage of the very attractively priced eight party line package

U.S. MAIL SERVICE:

The early Colonists were the recipients of the Rural Free Delivery Mail Service. Families on Lafayette Avenue were allowed to place their mail box along the road in front of their home. Families on Maple Street, Floral Avenue, School Avenue and Spring Street were obliged to cluster their mail box at the corner of Lafayette Avenue and their respective street. This all changed in the 1940's when Ben Rosen, a resident at the end of Floral Avenue, petitioned the U.S Mail service to provide mail delivery to each home. The house-to- house mail delivery began when Rosen assisted the U.S. Post Office in numbering all the previously unnumbered properties in the Colony

SCHOOL YARD JUSTICE:

Letting the air out of tires was the ultimate punishment. The teenage boys in the Colony had their own "Code of Justice." When wronged by another boy, the ultimate punishment was two flat tires on the perpetrator's bike

THE TIME LINE OF THE COLONY, FROM ITS INCEPTION TO ITS DISSOLUTION.

1921:   Bernard Somer begins his search for a Commuter Colony. Charlie Singawald, a Chatham Township native and a co-worker of Somer at the Prudential Insurance in Newark N.J "alerts" Somer to the Webster and Jennie Estes property on Lafayette Avenue, Chatham Township.

1921:   Early summer: Somer previews the property

1921:   The acquisition of the Estes property begins in July

1921:   Somer advertises in newspapers for potential members to form a Commuter Colony

1921:   October 13th: First meeting of potential members held at the Bertha Robbins N.Y.C. apartment. The purpose of the meeting was to visit the Estes property on October 16th, 1921

1921:   October 17th: Letter sent to Edward Lum, the attorney for the Estes family, indicating strong interest in the Estes property

1921:   October 19th: Letter sent to potential members describing the land. The letter originated by Bernard Somer, 1517 Washington Ave. Bronx, New York

1921:   December 6th: Letter sent to potential members outlining the goals of a Commuter Colony, and the accessibility to New York City. Twenty minute walk to trolley line to Newark, N.J. Delaware-Lackawanna trains to Newark and Hoboken N.J. The land is 234' above sea level

1922:   January 12th: Letter announcing a special meeting, December 15th, to act on a motion to take an option on the Estes property to establish a Commuter Colony and a Modern School. B. Somer, B Chafez and B. Robbins were selected for the "option" committee

1922:   January 26th: Letter announcing "important meeting" to discuss "do we go out to Chatham next spring or not". Terms of the sale are spelled out

1922:   February 1st: Letter announcing the necessity to raise the balance of the $750,00 to buy the option on the Estes property. The pledges will be called in on February 6th

1922:   March 2nd: Letter reports the committee agreed on the terms of the purchase, the adoption of a constitution and by-laws and the election of officers. The money has been raised to acquire the option

1922:   March 9th: Letter announcing that the Colony Association has purchased the option of the property as of March 6th

1922:   April 12th: Letter to members encouraging new potential members to join. Members invited to visit the site. Train fare is 65 cents

1922:   April 15th: Letter announcing the first general meeting. The purpose of the meeting is to raise the balance of the $10,000 necessary to take possession of the property before June 1st

1922:   April 15th: Letter calls for an April 22nd meeting to raise the $10,000 by June 15th to accelerate the possession of the land

1922:   April 22nd: Letter to the membership detailing the accomplishments of the committee. The official bank is the Fifth Avenue Branch of State Bank. Forty four members subscribed to sixty seven acres. $7,695 was raised toward the $10,000

1922:   May 2nd: Letter urging members to bring in the balance of their pledge toward the $10,000

1922:   May 24th: Letter announcing an excursion to the property

1922:   May 27th: The $10,000 deposit money is finally collected, in the bank and ready to be turned over to the Estes family, well before the June 15th deadline. The time to celebrate had come

1922:   June 24th: Letter announcing that general meetings will be held every two weeks instead of weekly

1922:   June 26th: Letter announcing the next meeting will be at The Peoples House at 7 East 15th Street, N.Y.C. A Mr. Wood is invited to discuss Colony problems

1922:   August 17th: Letter announcing the suspension of membership meetings until further notice, pending the clearance of the title. Attorneys for both the seller and the buyers are clearing up the objection raised by the Guaranty Company, namely, the location of a right of way

1922:   August 26th: The Chatham Press reports the delay in the passing of title has caused many rumors to circulate through the Township. Rumors to the effect, that the interlopers are unable to finalize the purchase of the property. Somer meets with the Chatham Press editor, and dispels all the rumors

1922:   September 7th: Letter announcing a special meeting to discuss the Consideration of Title. The Consideration of Title was the formality of putting in writing the, who, what, where and when of the existing contract

1922:   October 19th: Colony acquires the Estes property. This was the Colony's Fourth of July

1922:   October 25th: Letter to the membership announcing a dinner to celebrate the land acquisition

1922:   November 15th: Letter announcing the first meeting of The Chatham Colony Association, since the purchase of the Estes property, will be held at the Rand School, 7 East 15th Street, N.Y.C

1923:   Early spring: Colony purchases a tractor and begins clearing the land for the roads

1923:   Winter marked the arrival of the early pioneers. Hyman Rubin and Joseph Honexfeld survive the first winter

1924:   The first marriage takes place in the Colony. Louis Thorner takes Clair Morrison as his bride

1924:   Winter, a well and a 10,000 gallon tank are installed on Spring Street

1924:   Jersey Central Power and Light begins the installation of electricity in the Colony

1924:   The clearing of the land for the baseball field on the westerly side of the Colony

1925: The planning and the start of construction of the Community House on School Avenue

1928: June 5th: Public Service Electric and Gas purchases a swatch of land from the Colony to construct a power line

1928: The beginning of home deliveries of milk, bread, produce, ice and coal

1928: The first attempt of opening a store at 208, now 252, Lafayette Avenue

1928: The dredging and construction of the Colony Pool and bathhouse

1930: The Commonwealth Water Company agrees to provide water for the Colony

1932: Bernard Somer declares bankruptcy, loses his home through foreclosure, ends his ties with the Colony, and moves to Newark, N.J.

1933: July 17th: William {Valutchic} Kondrat becomes the first and only person to survive going through the rapids and the whirlpools at Niagara Falls, 1933. August 18th, 1933 Valutch comes home to a hero's welcome

1933: March 23rd: Morris Langer is assassinated in his garage by a bomb attached to the starter of his car.

1935: Lou Cohn accidently loses a leg boarding the Lackawanna train at the Chatham Station

1942: October 21st: Charlie Stuckelman is killed at the Norfolk Navel Base in Virginia

1943:   The Colonists opened the pool to non members of the Colony.The first lifeguard is hired. The membership fee for a family was $5.00 for the season

1950:   The Colony changes its minimum one acre restriction to a half acre minimum, to conform to the Township code

1954:   Senator Joseph McCarthy is brought before a Senate hearing to answer for his reckless unfounded list of communists in government and those in private life. Some Colonists felt they were on McCarthy's phantom list

1960:   Talk of dissolution of the Colony begins

1968:   December 5th: The Chatham Township Committee introduced a bond issue for the purpose of purchasing the Colony Pool and all of the assets of the Chatham Colony Association

1969:   January 1st: The formality of dissolution took place after forty seven years or to be more precise, 16,877 days.

CHATHAM COLONY, LEGAL DOCUMENTS

CONSTITUTION

OF THE

<u>CHATHAM COLONY ASSOCIATION</u>

PREAMBLE

The Chatham Colony Association is formed for the purpose of buying a tract of land near Chatham N.J, dividing it into parcels and selling the parcels to its members at cost price for the purpose of building homes and farming.

Among the aims of the Association is the establishment of a modern school for the education of children and of various facilities for the entertainment and education of its members and their quests.

1. NAME

The name of this Association is to be the Chatham Colony Association.

11. MEMBERSHIP

1. Any man or woman who is in sympathy with the aims of the association and who takes it upon himself or herself to comply

with the Constitution and By-Laws of this organization may become a member of the Association.

2. In order to become a member one must buy not less than one plot and more than three plots of land in the Colony organized by the Association.

3. Any one can remain a member of the Association only as long as he owns at least one plot of land in the Colony.

   Note: A plot is understood to be a parcel of land as indicated in a certified map made by a surveyor.

111. RIGHTS AND DUTIES OF THE MEMBERS

1. Each member obligates himself or herself to pay any and all of the taxes, dues and assessments decided upon by the general meeting of the association.

2. Each member after he has paid in full for his share of land and has met his other obligations toward the Association will be granted an individual title to his land when the Association comes into the full possession of the entire tract of land.

3. The land individually owned by a member of the Association in the Colony entitles him to a proportionate share in the communal land owned by the Association.

4. If a member fails to meet his obligations toward the Association within four [4] weeks, he forfeits all his rights to the land, and the Association, after due notice given by registered mail, has the right to sell the land the real property on the same. The proceeds of the sale, after deducting the amount due to the Association, are to be turned over by the Association, to the member. However, the

Association, in such a case, reserves for itself the right to keep the proceeds of the sale for a year.

5. A member has the right to sell his property in the Colony to anyone acceptable to the Association. The buyer then becomes a member of the Association and assumes all the privileges and duties of a member.

6. A member withdrawing from the Chatham Colony Association must give written notice to that effect either to the President or to the Recording Secretary of the Association.

7. If a withdrawing member wishes the Association to dispose for him of his holdings in the Colony, the Association shall charge him for this service 2% commission, which commission shall be donated to the School in the Colony.

CONTRIBUTION TOWARD THE MODERN SCHOOL BY THE CHATHAM COLONY ASSOCIATION

1. Five acres of land are set aside by the Chatham Colony Association for the purpose of establishing a modern school and a Social Center in the Colony.

2. Besides the donation of land, as provided above, members of the Chatham Colony Association shall not be taxed for the support of the School.

IV. BUILDINGS AND BUSINESS ENTERPRISES

1. No buildings whatsoever shall be erected within fifty [50] feet from the side of the road [the curb of the road].

2. Any business enterprises, outside of farming, may be opened only in a place approved of by the Association.

V. ASSESSMENTS AND DUES

1. All improvements, such as cutting of roads, the establishing of a water system, electric lighting, sidewalks, etc., will be installed. maintained and controlled by the Association, and the cost of installing and maintaining these improvements as well as all expenditures of the Association directly connected with the purchase and dividing of the land, shall be covered by assessment on the members in proportion to the number of plots they hold.

2. All expenses of the Association not attributed to the land are to be covered by special assessments paid equally by each member.

V1. MANAGEMENT

1. To conduct the business of the Association, the members at a general meeting elect officers, an Executive Committee and special committees.

2. The officers of the Association are: The President; the Vice President; the Recording Secretary; the Financial Secretary; three Trustees and two Auditors. No member can hold more than one office at one time.

3. The Executive Committee shall be composed of all the officers, except the auditors, and two additional members elected at the general meeting.

4. Special committees are to be elected for special purposes as the need of them may arise.

5. The Special Committees shall work in accord with the Executive Committee. In case of disagreement between the Executive and a special committee, the matter is to be settled by a general meeting of the membership.

V11. ELECTIONS

1. All members of the Executive Committee are to be elected for a period of one year; nomination and election to take place during the first week in May of every year.

2. The auditors are to be elected for a period of six [6] months, nomination and election to take place in May and November.

3. The Term of a Special Committee expires when their special work has been accomplished. In any event their term expires at the time when a new Executive Committee shall be elected.

4. All officers, members of the Executive and Special Committees can be recalled by a ¾ vote of the organization.

V111. GENERAL MEETINGS

1. Ordinary general meetings of the membership are to be held monthly.

2. Special general meetings shall be called by the Executive Committees, or the President, whenever necessity arises or upon the request of 10 or more members, of the Association made to the Executive Committee or the President.

IX. RIGHTS AND DUTIES OF THE EXECUTIVE COMMITTEE

1. The Executive Committee shall enforce all the laws of the Association and carry out all the resolutions adapted by the general meetings of the Association.

2. The Executive Committee has the right to extend time for payment to delinquent members. But in no case should such extension exceed six months.

3. The Executive Committee shall act as the guardian of affairs and interest of the Association in the interim between general meetings

4. The Executive Committee shall consider all applications for membership and submit its recommendations to the general meetings.

5. The Executive Committee shall have charge of all grievances coming before the Association.

X. DUTIES OF OFFICERS

A. THE PRESIDENT

1. The President shall preside at the meetings of the Executive Committee and act as ex-officio on all committees.

2. The President has the deciding vote in case of a tie.

3. The President, together with the Recording Secretary, shall sign all contracts and agreements entered into by the Association.

B. VICE-PRESIDENT

The Vice-President shall perform the duties of the President in case of his disability or absence.

C. RECORDING SECRETARY

1. The Recording Secretary shall attend all general meetings of the Association as well as the meetings of the Executive Committee and keep a true record of their proceedings. He shall keep a list of all members, their names, addresses, and conduct all the correspondence of the Association.

2. The Recording Secretary shall have charge of the Seal of the Association and together with the President, sign all contracts and agreements entered into by the Association.

D. FINANCIAL SECRETARY

1. The Financial Secretary shall receive all moneys due the Association for which he shall issue proper receipts. The money received he shall turn over immediately to the Treasurer.

2. The Financial Secretary shall keep a set of books where the members' accounts and all the other accounts of the Association shall be entered. He shall balance the books for each calendar month and have them ready for auditing within the first week of the following month.

3. The Financial Secretary shall notify all members in arrears of their indebtedness to the Association.

4. At any time, upon request, the Financial Secretary shall submit for examination to the Auditors, the President or the Trustees, all the books and files in his charge belonging to the Association.

5. The Financial Secretary shall be bonded for the sum of One Thousand Dollars, [$1,000.00].

E. THE TREASURER

1. The Treasure shall receive all the moneys turned over to him by the Financial Secretary to whom he shall issue receipts. All moneys thus received shall be deposited by the Treasurer in the Bank in the name of the Chatham Colony Association, Inc, subject to be drawn by check signed by the Treasurer, the President and one of the Trustees.

2. The Treasurer shall pay by check all bills ordered paid by the general membership meeting or by the Executive Committee.

3. The Treasurer shall keep an account book wherein receipts and disbursements shall be entered. This book shall be balanced for each calendar month, and it must be ready for auditing within the first week of the following month.

   At any time, upon request, the Treasurer shall submit for examination to the auditors, the President or the Trustees, all the books and files in his charge belonging to the Association.

4. The Treasurer shall be bonded for the sum of One Thousand Dollars [1,000.00].

F. THE AUDITORS

Within the first two weeks of each month, the Auditors shall audit all the books, accounts, receipts, vouchers, bills, statements, etc., for the preceding calendar month, and report on their findings to the general membership meeting.

G. THE TRUSTEES

The Trustees shall have general charge of all the funds and properties of the Association. They shall see to it that all moneys in charge of the Treasurer exceeding $200.00, be deposited in the bank. They shall examine all bills and books concerning the Association and report upon the same whenever they find it necessary.

AMENDMENTS TO THE CONSTITUTION

The Constitution can be amended by a 3/4 vote at a special meeting called for the purpose where not less than 2/3 of the membership are present.

Copies of the proposed amendments to be distributed to the members two weeks before action is taken.

THE CHATHAM COLONY CONTRACT FOR MEMBERS USING THE COLONY WATER SUPPLY

RULES

regulating the supply of water from the Water System established and maintained by the Chatham Colony Association, Inc. Approved at the General Meeting of the Association held on August 28th, 1927.

A. GENERAL REGULATIONS

1. Any owner of property in the Colony who is not over three months behind in payments due to the Colony, and who has not violated the covenants to which the property is subjected, has the right to be connected to the water system and use the water upon payment of the fixed charges.

2. To secure the satisfactory function of the water system and the proper distribution of water to the users, there shall be elected every year by the General Meeting of the Association a permanent Water Committee of two members. The duties of this committee are: to supervise all work connected with the water system, to issue permits for the connection of pipes to, or for their disconnection from the water mains, to enforce all the rules and regulations for the water users, to keep records of all water charges and report same to the Financial Secretary for collection.

3. Any one desiring to install a water supply must, through the Water Committee, apply for a permit to the Executive Committee of Chatham Colony Association, Inc.

4. All water users are obliged to install water meters, supplied by the Chatham Colony Association at cost. The installation of the water meter is at the user's expense.

5. The installation of the water meter as well as the connecting of water pipes to the main must be either done by one authorized by the Water Committee, or inspected and approved by the authorized person before covering. The same applies to all repairs or changes made at any place between the water main and the meter.

6. All water pipes must be buried at least three and a half feet beneath the ground.

7. Water must be shut off in the winter in all unoccupied or unheated buildings. Failure to comply with this ruling carries with it a penalty of $25. Besides the charge for damages and repairs in case of leakage or freezing of the pipes.

8. It is understood that by being connected to the water system any owner of property in the Colony expressly agrees that the premises may be entered in his or her absence by members of the Water Committee or by those authorized by the same for the purpose of reading the meter or inspection, also for the purpose of turning off the water or making urgently needed repairs in case of emergency.

B. CHARGES

1. Everyone connected to the Water System is to pay a service charge of fifty cents per month for each connection to the main, no matter whether water was used or not. The charge to be collected for all the months passed from January 1st, 1927 which, likewise, applies to those having been or going to be connected after that date.

2.   The collected service charge shall provide the means to cover the cost of large repairs and replacement of machinery.

3.   In addition to the service charge, those using the water must pay a certain price per 100 cubic feet, which price shall be calculated to cover the ordinary expenses of running the water system, including small repairs.

4.   The basic price per 100 cubic feet of water shall be fixed every year by the general meeting of the Association upon recommendation of the Water Committee, the calculation to be based on the cost of running the water system and the amount of water used in the preceding year.

5.   Those using more than 100 cubic feet of water per month shall be allowed the following reduction in price:

On the first 100 cubic feet- no reduction
    : second :   : -10% :
    : third   :   : -20% :
    : fourth :   : -30% :
    : fifth   :   : - 40% :
    : sixth and above   : - 50% :

6.   Those using the water without having installed water meters shall pay $1.00 per month, above all other charges, the Water Committee to fix the quantity of the water used by estimation.

C MEASURES TO SECURE PAYMENT

1.   Bills for the water connection and for the used water shall be presented every three months. Such bills are due upon presentation.

2. If any owner of property in the Colony is over three months behind in payments due to the Colony for the yearly assessment, for water connection or for used water, and after having been given proper notice, fails to make good the delinquency with in a month, the Executive Committee may cause the water connection to be cut off. Reconnection shall be allowed only upon payment of the amount due plus cost of disconnection.

HIGHLIGHTS

ACKNOWLEDGEMENTS WITH APPRECIATION

The list of people contacted for input and verification of information.

Irving Weiss, An amazing source of Colony history

Beatrice Katz Philwin

Blanche Thorner Blumenfeld

Valaria Kondrat Anjoorian

Bailey Brower: Descendent of the Noe dynasty

Mitzi Eisenscher

Alex Koukley

Estelle Stuckleman Greenberg

Damien Jacobs

Kristin Abromitis Jacobs

Riva Sheib Kramer

Milton Abbazia

Diana Abbazia Holdridge

Isadore Blumen

Robert Headley

Frieda Abbazia, Information retrieved 32 years after her death from a recording made in 1978.

The Morris County Hall of Records Staff

Bernard Mollod

Carol Muth

Carolyn Knott, Chatham Township Historical Society

Ruth Baltteim Olson

Parklane Photo and Imaging, Photo restoration. a "big" thank you.

BIOGRAPHY

**Bert Abbazia and the beautiful Theresa Romano on their wedding day –
October 9, 1949.**

ABOUT THE AUTHOR

Bert Abbazia was born the second son of Oreste and Frieda Somer Abbazia,
original Colony members, on August 14th, 1927. He is the "product" of
what in 1927 was considered a mixed marriage. His father had been
a practicing Catholic in his formative years while his mother was an
agnostic Romanian Jew. He enjoyed a happy, carefree childhood growing

up surrounded by nature's gifts at 252 Lafayette Avenue in the Colony section of Chatham Township. Bert earned eleven varsity letters and received All State recognition for Soccer and Basketball while at Chatham High School. Upon his graduation he enlisted in the U.S Navy at age seventeen and served on the USS Houston during World War 11. August 14th became a significant day in the author's life. Not only was August 14th his birth date, it was the day Japan surrendered in 1945 and the day Bert was honorably discharged in 1946. Within two weeks after his discharge he enrolled at Seton Hall College. The year, 1949, saw Bert start Done-Well Cleaners, graduate Seton Hall University and marry his high school sweetheart. He and his wife Theresa are the proud parents of three daughters, six grandchildren and six great grandchildren.

With each passing year he came to the realization that "the environment and the circumstances" surrounding his upbringing were unique. "Here is a story that was waiting to be told and I had to tell it!"